PRAISE FOR THE FIRST EDITION (

"*Over Goal!* is one of the best books to
– practical, comprehensive, and insightful.

> Charles W. Collier, Senior Philanthropic Adviser
> *Harvard University*

"Reading *Over Goal!* is like enjoying a series of leisurely
lunches with a brilliant, wise, and down to earth fundraiser.
Almost invisibly, Kay Sprinkel Grace transfers a philosophy
and sense of fundraising."

> Jan Masaoka, President and CEO
> *Compasspoint Nonprofit Services*

"Well known for her insight on fundraising and board
development, Kay Sprinkel Grace shares that insight in *Over
Goal!* in the form of practical advice for managing a
fundraising program."

> Paulette Maehara, President and CEO
> *Association of Fundraising Professionals*

"In pages rich with practical advice, Kay Sprinkel Grace's
wisdom, experience, and willingness to think outside the box
come shining through. *Over Goal!* will recharge the batteries
of dedicated leaders everywhere."

> Mike Cortés, Director
> *Institute for Nonprofit Organization Management*
> *University of San Francisco*

"*Over Goal!* is a handy guide for meeting today's challenges
in nonprofit fundraising. Kay Sprinkel Grace's is a voice of
accumulated experience and wisdom, relevant and up to date,
coaching you to sustained success in fundraising."

> Timothy Seiler, Director
> *The Fund Raising School*
> *The Center on Philanthropy at Indiana Univ.*

OVER GOAL!

**What You Must Know
To Excel at Fundraising Today**

First printed in September 2006

Printed in the United States of America

ISBN 1-889102-28-8

10 9 8 7 6 5 4 3 2

This text is printed on acid-free paper.

*Copies of this book are available from the
publisher at discount when purchased in
quantity for boards of directors or staff.*

*Emerson & Church, Publishers
P.O. Box 338 • Medfield, MA 02052
Tel. 508-359-0019 • www.emersonandchurch.com*

Library of Congress Cataloging-in-Publication Data

Grace, Kay Sprinkel.
  Over goal! : what you must know to excel at fundraising today
/ Kay Sprinkel Grace. — 2nd ed., rev. & enl.
     p. cm.
Includes index
  ISBN 1-889102-28-8 (pbk. : alk. paper)
  1. Fund raising. 2. Nonprofit organizations—Finance. 3.
Boards of directors. I. Title.
  HV41.2.G726 2006
  658.15'224—dc22

                                    2006023937

Expanded & Revised Second Edition

OVER GOAL!

What You Must Know to Excel at Fundraising Today

KAY SPRINKEL GRACE

Emerson
& Church
PUBLISHERS

THE AUTHOR

Kay Sprinkel Grace is a prolific writer, creative thinker, inspiring speaker, and reflective practitioner. Her passion for philanthropy and its capacity to transform donors, organizations, and communities is well-known in the U.S. and internationally.

With an increasingly powerful vision for the way in which organizations, funders, and communities must partner to resolve community problems and enhance cultural, educational, and other resources, Kay has increased the understanding and motivation of donors and organizations regarding the importance of the philanthropic sector in today's changing and challenging society.

She lives in San Francisco and is an enthusiastic photographer, traveler, hiker, and creative writer. When not writing, speaking, or consulting, you can find her with her children and grandchildren who live in San Francisco, upstate New York, and France.

This book is dedicated to my son, friend, and professional colleague, Greg. His multi-dimensional and untiring support has given me space, time, and inspiration to reflect and write.

CONTENTS

INTRODUCTION

Part I: Fundraising

Part II: Board and Organizational Development

INTRODUCTION

It's a new world for nonprofit organizations. The 21st century began with a bang, creating even more demands for responsive and innovative programs and services.

Communities are looking increasingly at nonprofits to partner with them to address new or continuing needs in education, health, the environment, arts and culture, and the many causes that address other social or quality of life needs.

Government funding, which began eroding in the U.S. and globally in the 1980s, hasn't been restored and, with the dramatically volatile economy, corporate and foundation funding has also become less stable.

While individuals remain the largest source of funding in the U.S., and many are also investing overseas, the overall outlook is one where the need for nonprofit services is exceeding the optimism about how to fund them.

And, the practice of fundraising is changing more rapidly than ever. More sophisticated donors, expecting accountability, transparency, and disclosure, are demanding new performance standards. Competition is stiff, with many organizations vying for the same limited dollars and seemingly addressing the same community needs. Donors are asking for more clarity, collaboration, and evidence of good management.

On the governance side, volunteers seem to be in short supply, and the board members everyone want to recruit are over-committed.

If these are the realities, what are the best strategies for creating new performance standards for nonprofits? How can we meet donors and client demands, build boards that will have energy and vision, and navigate the rough waters of a new century and a seemingly new economy?

This book was written to address these issues in common sense language. It is drawn from my experience as a development professional and consultant for nearly 30 years, and from an additional 20 years as a volunteer leader.

While the primary focus is on fundraising, the book honors the fundamental truth that without good governance, fundraising is nearly impossible. The chapters on governance are as important as the chapters on fundraising. The two functions are inseparable.

My own view of the future of philanthropy and nonprofits is very optimistic. I feel that America's voluntary sector activities – and the ways in which they've been carried overseas as our most meaningful social export – have never been more poised to have a powerful impact on society.

I invite all of you to learn more about how you can meet and exceed your goals, increase your impact, and stay comfortably ahead of the waves of change.

San Francisco, Calif.   Kay Sprinkel Grace

Part One

FUNDRAISING

1

Successful Nonprofit Organizations

Donors invest in them. Talented professionals want to work for them. The media cover their activities. The community talks about them. And you know and admire (and maybe even envy) them.

They are the successful organizations in your community that attract money, publicity, and leadership while other organizations wonder why.

They can be small, medium, or large. They may work in the arts, social services, medical care, or any of the other critical areas served by the public benefit sector. And they need not be venerable to be perceived as valuable: new organizations with a compelling vision and a mission that reflects an unmet community need will attract leaders, funders, and professionals.

So what are the secrets?

Here is what's important to know about the qualities, practices, and attributes of successful nonprofit organizations.

Unwavering vision.

Through good times and bad, up cycles and downturns,

stability and change, the vision of their leadership – and their commitment to working towards that vision – doesn't falter.

One medical center, suffering from the whipsaw of two mergers, financial hemorrhages, and public resistance to philanthropic support for already-expensive care, is now thriving again.

The center raises between $13 and $15 million each year in annual support and planned gifts while other centers in the same community founder.

What is the reason? Unwavering vision. The board stayed with the organization and continued to advocate for its merits as an investment. The foundation staff, undergoing its own merger and transition, kept its vision strong and its leadership was untiring. And the new CEO is a trusted physician who is bold, trustworthy, and able to build confidence.

It remains the most admired medical center in the community and, among all kinds of organizations, is one of the most distinguished.

Confidence.

Confidence begets confidence.

Organizations that are confident of the integrity of their mission, the quality of their vision, and their ability to deliver programs and services are far more attractive to investors than those constantly apologizing for the sector, for their lack of resources, or for their performance. As a result, investors gain confidence and continue to support these organizations.

A very small theater company was determined to take its unique performances overseas. Confident of receiving foundation funding for the trip, the theatre group was disappointed when its request was denied.

But the setback didn't deter the group. They enlisted a friend who knew the funder. She was convinced that the performers and the artistic director had an excellent product and would fulfill the aspirations of the foundation if given the opportunity.

The funder relented, provided the grant and now – seven years later – is still supporting the company for its now annual performance tours overseas.

That success has attracted other funders and given the company a visibility and reputation that's reflected in increased attendance and support.

No mission drift.

Mission drift, that dangerous condition whereby organizations focus more intently on their own internal issues rather than issues in the community, kills success. Passion has to be fanned and fed.

Board members usually stop serving when they feel no connection to the mission, and funders stop investing in groups whose entire message is about their organizational issues and difficulties (including shortfalls) rather than the impact they're making in the community.

Public benefit corporations exist for the public benefit: be sure you're looking through your windows into the community, and not just into mirrors, when you do your planning, fundraising, and recruitment. Talk about the needs you're meeting, not the needs you have.

Clarity of values.

With successful organizations, there's no doubt about what they value. It's woven into their vision, frames their mission, and guides their staff and volunteers.

But it's one thing to speak values and another to evidence them through everything you do.

The major success of Sage Hill School in Orange County,

an independent high school, is largely attributable to its comfort with and dedication to integrating its values into every aspect of its operations: board recruitment, fundraising, choice of faculty, admission of students, curriculum, disciplinary, and other standards.

Marketing and enrollment materials sing with the freshness and clarity of the school's values-based approach to education and community involvement. Banners with words like "Commitment," "Excellence," "Integrity," "Community," and others fly from the interior roofline.

As I was visiting the campus one day, a young man told me how much he liked being a student there. We chatted about his reasons and then, looking up at the banners, he pointed and said, "I got that award last year." Not seeing which one he meant, I asked. "Integrity," he said. And when I asked him to define integrity, he said: "It means being true to others and true to yourself." A good lesson for a 17-year-old and for all of us.

Sage Hill raised $34 million for its initial campus plan and scholarships and now, several years after its founding, is entering into plans for continued expansion and scholarship support. The board remains dedicated to the vision, and the values are prevalent in the classroom, in its service learning programs, even on the playing fields.

A sense of abundance.

Successful organizations don't whine. They realize that philanthropy comes from abundance, and they're instrumental in creating a sense of abundance among those who use their services, fund their programs, and give time as volunteers.

An organization I know that houses and provides job training and child care for the working poor and homeless is fast-becoming one of the most successful organizations in the community.

Its administrative facilities are modest, its mission difficult, its successes often hard to measure. But the organization realizes that its impact isn't really in numbers, it is in lives.

The group has captured that as their measure of abundance. At their annual dinner – attended by nearly a thousand people in the community – there was hushed attention paid as a young woman who has benefited from the program spoke of her vision for herself and others like her, and told not of what she didn't have but of what she'd been given by this program: hope.

While other organizations that serve this same population tend to focus on their needs, this one focuses on the needs it's meeting and must meet. Their spirit of abundance has been contagious, and the interest of high-profile leaders and donors in the community is growing.

Courage.

A strong attribute of leaders, courage also characterizes organizations. Courage to lead and to know when to follow. Courage to take calculated risks if the result will advance the mission. Courage to make tough decisions about people, ideas, and programs.

A much-loved but badly managed organization tried in vain to keep its doors open. Revelations about its true financial condition began to emerge and the executive director (and nearly the entire staff) had to step down.

Community outreach for funding and support rallied for a while, but ultimately it was clear the organization had run its course.

One board member, with extensive corporate experience, stepped forward and led the process of phasing out the organization. Sadness, agony, and remorse accompanied the courageous determination to close the doors with dignity and honor.

Other similar organizations stepped forward to embrace its members, and the board can feel good about the process and the results even as it mourns the loss of this community resource.

Short of having to muster the courage to close, the courage of successful organizations is most often seen in decisions to take a stand on a particular program that's threatened, or to "de-enlist" board members who no longer have interest, or to evaluate and dismiss employees who aren't fulfilling the mission.

Transparency and regular communication.

Transparency is a watchword, not a buzzword.

Successful organizations remain successful by being transparent about mission, performance, *and* problems. Their board and staff communicate with one another, and with donors and the community. Their newsletters don't feature board members having parties: they tell stories and present statistics about the impact they're having in the community.

The story above of the organization closing its doors is an excellent example of failure to be transparent. The staff withheld even from the board the true financial picture – if they hadn't, the closing might have been averted. Donors weren't informed of the true situation. Neither were vendors.

Pride often blocks our willingness to be transparent. But as we increasingly view contributions as investments, it's even more necessary to be transparent with our investors. The two bottom lines of the public benefit sector are gauged in return on values and return on investment (and by the later I don't mean a financial return, but the knowledge that the money is handled well and invested wisely).

An emphasis on donor development, not just fund raising.

Annual
Appeal

Successful organizations spend time and money on developing relationships, not just on raising money. Donor development is the key function in successful fundraising, and yet too often we say we don't have time or money to cultivate and steward our donors.

One of the lessons we learn from our friends in the corporate sector is that it's easier to reactivate an existing "customer" than to find a new one. We need only to look at the cost of donor acquisition, as opposed to renewal, to know that is true for our sector as well.

Make the case for a budget allocation to cultivate your prospects and steward your donors. When you focus on relationships and donor development, the money will follow.

Continual planning.

I'm always amazed when I receive a call from an organization saying it needs a new plan, that its five-year plan is nearly up.

If you use the "rolling base" process – one requiring an annual evaluation of your current year's progress and the addition of another year to the plan – this won't happen.

Then, only every three to five years will you need to conduct a zero-based process that extensively surveys your organization and the marketplace.

Those whom we draw on for leadership and who are successful in business, finance, and government increasingly expect us to have a sound planning and evaluation process.

Respect, camaraderie and fun.

Successful organizations have respect for each other at the staff level, respect for volunteers including board members, a sense of team commitment, and the time and permission to play.

Ours is serious work, but we don't have to make it a drill.

21

One organization, barely making payroll and budget for a while, nonetheless had weekly celebrations (with beer and pizza provided by a board member). Why? Because they made it through another week.

That was nearly 20 years ago, and today the agency is thriving. Why? Because they felt like a team, played like a team and celebrated like a team.

Another organization I'm familiar with, a successful children's services agency, can attribute much of its success to the integrated way in which board and staff work as a team.

One therapist, working tirelessly with an autistic child who for years came close to speaking but couldn't cross that threshold, came running out of her office one day shouting, "He talked! He talked!" The next day, her fellow staff members had a T-shirt ready for her which she proudly wore. It said, "Damn I'm Good."

Board members and other volunteers became aware of this, and the accomplishment gave them the idea of having a staff appreciation event. It has become a tradition.

This continues to be an organization that attracts top community leaders and major funders – and it's more than 50 years since it was founded.

•••

If you want to be successful, start thinking success. Focus on your abundance, not your shortfalls, and focus on the people who make your work possible: those who lead, those who fund, and those you serve.

2

Positioning Your Organization as a Solid Investment

"If you always do what you've always done, you'll always be what you've always been." *Anonymous*

While ordinarily applied to the ruts we get into in our own lives, that little saying applies to nonprofit organizations as well.

If we're to meet the market demand for our services and the increasing expectations of our donors, we have to start doing things differently. And, we need to let our constituencies know we're making changes based on what we perceive as their needs.

There is an ironic aspect to our organizations that's becoming more obvious as the pace of society quickens. It is this. We are change agents, yet we're extraordinarily slow to change.

Part of this is due to our governance structure – gaining (volunteer) board consensus requires much more discussion than the corporate model of governance. Another contributor is our lack of resources. We simply don't have the resources to devote to enhancing and increasing the effectiveness of our governance.

But if we are to remain competitive, we need to begin

23

adjusting our systems and structure to be more flexible, more accountable, and more attractive to our investors.

Here are important things to know for positioning your organization as an attractive, sturdy, and vibrant investment.

Be transparent.

The mystique of separateness that surrounded nonprofits in the 1970s, 80s, and even into the 90s has been stripped away. We're now expected to be able partners with the corporate and government sectors in building our communities.

Because we exist in the public trust, we must be open with our vision, governance, and finances. Major donors aren't going to invest in an organization which they know little about.

Drawn to the issues we address, and inspired by the passion those issues generate, investors need to know how we're managing their investment, what impact that investment is having, and the overall progress of our efforts towards addressing the issues they're concerned about.

Be accessible.

People with money but little experience in philanthropy complain that they'd like to give, but organizations don't respond either quickly enough or clearly enough.

A donor concerned about an issue views your agency as a vehicle for solving a problem (human or societal) or enhancing particular resources (cultural, artistic, educational). If you don't respond, the donor will go to another (and another) until a responsive organization is found.

One donor confided recently that he'd "given up" trying to give money around a particular issue because he "got the run-around" from every organization he contacted.

Our structure, lack of adequate management, and sometimes

poor systems deter people who are willing investors but unfamiliar with how to access us. Demystify the process. Let people know what you do and how they can help. Keep it simple: provide a 1-2-3 step guide in your literature or on your website.

Invest in good management - it will pay enormous returns.

Although it's important to keep your staff funding ratio strongly weighted towards those who deliver your program, it's equally important to have a CEO and management team with expertise, passion, and proven management skills.

The previously perceived gulf between nonprofit and for-profit management skill-sets is now largely ignored: major donors are looking for nonprofit managers with the ability to perform and respond like the corporate managers with whom they may be more familiar.

Under-investing in the administrative and financial management of your organization can cost you far more than you save ... in lost gifts and lost opportunities.

Evaluate how well the management and governance structure is working in your organization.

The way in which nonprofits are governed is based on state laws and is therefore fairly formulaic. A few well-known models have been tried, written about, and either kept or rejected. In evaluating the literature on governance, it may be time for the sector as a whole to consider whether the basic governance structure of nonprofits really works in the 21st century.

Executive directors are burning out at forest fire rates, and development directors are diminishing in number. Even program directors, fueled by the passion of their work, find the board/staff balance a difficult one, and are concerned about keeping it appropriate.

For an investor, these issues can be critical. Within the parameters of your state laws and your own by-laws, take time to evaluate whether there's a better model of governance for your organization, one allowing it to respond to change and opportunity more readily.

Stay relevant.

Because nonprofits are values and vision driven, they can fall into the trap where their programs (or at least the description of them) can seem irrelevant to a changing community. Further, we compound the problem when we position ourselves as "charities" rather than "investments."

If we consider ourselves charities, we're in danger of adopting an outlook whereby we feel people are obligated to invest in us. Nothing could be further from the truth. You're competing for the investment of discretionary funds – nonprofits are another form of community investment.

On your website, in your printed materials, and on every public occasion, convey why your organization and its programs – venerable and trusted or new and exciting – are highly relevant to the constantly emerging needs of your community.

Keep your mission fresh by framing it with current statistics about the marketplace: for example, how many children need therapy for learning disabilities, how many adolescents have turned to drugs.

Organizations cannot be lulled by their own successes. After all, "if we always do what we've always done...."

When you do change, let it be known.

Slow to change because of our structure and systems, we should be quick to let our constituents and investors know when we have changed and the probable impact of that change.

News about thoughtful and responsive change raises the perception people have of our organizations – we find ourselves described as "cutting edge" and "innovative" rather than stagnant or traditional.

Soon, that public perception can begin to shift the way people on the inside view the organization and lead to improved performance.

Use the best technology you can afford to communicate with the public.

The cost of being current with new media and technology drifts downwards every day. It's no longer a luxury to have a website or email – it's a necessity. To be accessible, and viewed as an organization in the mainstream (or ahead of the wave), you need to have technology that works.

Further, if you're going to invest in a website, invest in a web master as well. Nothing is more off-putting to a potential donor than visiting your website in September and finding it hasn't been updated since May. Likewise, if you have an email link, be sure you respond.

Major gifts seldom come in via email, but the seed is often planted when someone visits your website and makes an inquiry. From that point on, it's up to you.

Make all your reports for finance and development ones that you're proud to share.

Accuracy in gift reporting and acknowledgment lays the foundation for good stewardship.

Without this basic attention to good records and good reporting, all the stewardship in the world (events, plaques, notes) won't encourage further involvement.

Be proud and positive that you're part of the most dynamic philanthropic era in history.

We are professionals and volunteers in rare times. Our sector is performing well in chaotic change, and it can perform better. The pay-off for higher performance is more investment from major donors. They're looking for good places to invest their money and to help their communities thrive. Become that place.

•••

In sum, position your organization as a place where vision and goals are well-communicated internally and externally, and where the sense of making a sound investment is keen.

3

Creating or Revising A Mission Statement

We talk about the importance of "mission-driven" fundraising. Yet, most organizations have mission statements describing what the group does, not why it does it. As a result, they miss a critical opportunity.

Potential donors are drawn by the values you convey. They sense a mutual benefit when they support you and the causes that concern them: health, music, art, social welfare, culture, children, senior services.

But within these causes are implicit values: dignity, independence, enrichment of life, the transcending power of art, the impact of science and discovery, fulfilling human potential.

When these values are conveyed in mission statements and marketing materials, there's an even more compelling rationale for those wanting to better their communities through philanthropy.

A mission statement that exemplifies this is the following. It was written nearly 15 years ago by the then-executive director, Karen Angel, when she was challenged in a fundraising class to express why her Eureka, California organization, one that provides medical intervention for injuries to hands, exists:

> "Next to the human face, hands are our most expressive feature. We talk with them. We work with them. We play with them. We comfort and love with them. An injury to the hand affects people both professionally and personally. At Vector Health Programs, we give people back the use of their hands."

A values-expressive mission statement like this is ultimately more motivating to both external and internal audiences than one simply describing what the organization does. It can set the stage for inquiry, interest, and involvement by volunteers and donors who are capable of making long-term investments of time and money.

Here, then, are important things to know about creating or revising a mission statement so that it becomes a compelling invitation for those who share your values.

Getting people focused on values isn't easy.

The literature on mission statements has pushed nonprofits to imitate their corporate counterparts, even to applying such constricting rules as "it needs to fit on the back of a business card" or be "25 words or less." Even more constraining is the companion belief that it must tell what you do, not why you do it.

To get to the essential "why," you have to focus on what your organization values. One way to begin is to conduct an exploratory session with your board and staff. Ask them to write down and discuss the three things they believe the organization values.

You'll get some key words and phrases like "dignity," "belief in human potential," "commitment to kids," "the power of music to transform lives," "a stronger community," "a hunger-free city."

Next, ask them to think about your current messages and materials. Are the values explicit or implicit? Do people have to work to get beyond the words that describe what you do (" ... provide food for agencies that have feeding programs") to why you do it? ("Hunger hurts. It erodes human dignity, drains human energy, and diminishes human potential.").

Once you've identified the values, the process can begin.

Gauge the tolerance of your leadership and the community for a mission statement that overtly conveys values.

If this approach to mission statements represents a sea change for your organization, the benefit of a values statement must be conveyed.

One approach is to explain to your board and volunteers that all voluntary giving (time, money, resources) is based in values; and that in order to become true investors in your work, people must understand what you stand for.

Although corporations may craft short and emotionless mission statements, they convey their values in the way they market their products. Automobile ads play to our needs for comfort, power, and distinction. Household product ads imply values-implicit consequences for not using them. Ice cream ads focus on self-reward as a reason for nightly raids to the freezer.

Because fundraising is a marketing process, we have to find ways to weave our values into the principal statement that expresses our mission, even if initial board and staff resistance is keen.

The content of a mission statement should be generated by a group but written by one person.

Once the values have been identified, and your staff and

board have made initial attempts at writing, assign the task of expanding (or distilling) the ideas and polishing the phrasing to a good writer who understands your values.

The results of "group write" are usually awkward. In mission statements, economy of language is critical, and each word should have purpose.

Yale University School of Medicine created this short statement for a campaign conducted in the early 1980s when the innovations in biomedical research were just starting:

"We are in the midst of one of the most profound intellectual revolutions of all time, the revolution in the biological sciences. Its implications for understanding life processes and for combating disease are boundless. Yale is in the forefront of this revolution."

The ideas were given to an outside writer. The result was exceptional. Although brief, it is rich in values and persuasive in tone.

Once the first draft is ready, test it out on selected internal and external constituencies.

If you send your statement to too many, the process will stall. Choose a sampling from board members, major donors, program staff, fundraising volunteers, and clients. You may even have a few versions to try out on them.

Set the criteria for them by explaining the importance of a mission statement that embodies the organization's values. If they weren't part of the process that led to the writing of the statement, summarize what you've done thus far. Provide them with a deadline for giving feedback, and a guideline for responding.

You may be delightfully surprised by the ideas that come back. Even one or two can make a big difference. You won't hear from everyone, but nearly all of those contacted will remember that you asked them. It is a process that promotes ownership of the eventual statement.

Test the statement by checking whether it answers the question, "Why do we exist?"

From the first brainstorming to the final writing, see if the ideas being generated complete the sentence, "We exist because...." For example, "We exist because hunger hurts." "We exist because people need their hands to work, play, love, and talk." "We exist because the biological sciences provide answers to critical life issues."

One community music education organization, searching deeply for its why, answered the challenge this way: "We exist because we cannot imagine a world without music."

If your mission statement is still stuck in "what," you won't be able to finish the sentence, "Why do we exist?" In truth, what we do and how we do it may change to adapt to the times, technology or our resources – but *why* we serve our community is less apt to change.

When the mission statement is tested, be sure it inspires as well as describes.

An occasional outbreak of goosebumps is healthy. It reminds people of the impact of their organization on human needs and potential. The hands statement, quoted earlier, brings goosebumps. Strangely, so does the Yale statement for me.

A happy outcome of reading such a statement is the sense of "Aha!" The reader feels she clicks with your values. The basis for a new or enhanced relationship has been discovered.

Remember that mission and vision aren't the same, and are often confused.

Mission describes the human or societal need you're meeting. Vision describes the community impact your organization will have when you succeed. A program developed to complement the work of Head Start in New Orleans has a vision statement that says it all: "Our vision is that every child in the greater New Orleans area will be ready when it is time to start school."

Jane Stanford, co-founder of Stanford University, wrote the following when the then-regional university was in the depths of financial peril following the death of her husband and the devastating 1906 San Francisco earthquake: "I can see a hundred years ahead, when all the present trials are forgotten ... The children's children's children, coming here from the east, the west, the north and the south."

At the university's Centennial in the early 1990s, her vision of a widely known and mature university was revisited with a sense of pride and fulfillment.

Not everyone is comfortable with values statements, so keep a "what" statement in reserve.

Just as those close to your organization may resist the values thrust of this type of mission statement, so, too, may some of your funders or other external constituents.

Keep a "what" statement handy. In fact, most mission statements written in the way described here are short paragraphs followed by longer statements that describe what the organization does. A funder may only wish to read the more traditional descriptive information.

Use it or lose it.

Adapt it, play with it, draw from it, be creative. Rearrange the words for various purposes: brochures, tag lines on stationery, donor thank you receipts, remit envelopes, signage in your administrative offices or where you see your clients.

Writing it is not enough – you have to live the values, too.

A statement behind a receptionist's desk is nice, but living the mission is what counts. Express your organization's values in what you do, how you do it, the decisions you make, and the way you treat people internally and in the community.

This will help prevent "mission drift," a problem that occurs when the board becomes more consumed with the institution's internal needs than with the external need that is being addressed.

•••

Creating or revising your mission statement is a worthy exercise for rekindling values and getting board members inspired.

A mission statement that tells "why" invites those who share your values to become more involved. It signals your community that you understand your true mission. It inspires your board and helps prevent "mission drift." It provides the values base for tough decision-making, and it is the source of other expressions of your mission that you'll develop for ongoing fundraising and community outreach.

4

The Role of Organizational Culture in Fundraising

When Tom Peters and Bob Waterman went in search of excellence years ago, one of the many things they discovered was the significant role of corporate culture.

Describing it as both the hardest and the softest aspect of organizations, they cited its role in determining behavior, performance, and perception.

Peters and Waterman drew on the work of Terrence E. Deal and Allen F. Kennedy, whose book, *Corporate Cultures*, had stirred up the organizational behavior community some years before.

Deal and Kennedy had identified myths, rituals, heroes, and celebrations among their corporate culture markers – and those of us in the nonprofit sector know just how strong these markers are! Not only do we see them evidenced in management practices, they're apparent in the way we raise money as well.

Culture is the DNA of organizations. The more we know about it, the more we're able to live with its ramifications and predict certain behaviors. And, when we attempt to alter practices in order to make changes, we have to begin by acknowledging not only its power, but the time and skill it takes to make significant changes.

Everyone a fundraiser

If Deal and Kennedy took a look at corporate culture as it's reflected in nonprofit fundraising practices, they would certainly identify the following.

If the board hasn't been recruited to raise money, don't expect to change their behavior quickly.

In his autobiography, Lee Iacocca reflected on his experience at Chrysler by saying that to change the culture, you have to change the people. He could have been speaking about the challenge of persuading a board that hasn't been recruited to raise money that they will love doing so!

To be sure, Iacocca had a distinct advantage: he could fire the vice presidents at Chrysler when he took over, thereby changing the culture. Most of us cannot – and would not want to – "fire" the board.

Even if you currently need a board active in fundraising, you still have to respect that this wasn't part of their job description. The first thing to do, obviously, is to change that description so that "participation in the fund and donor development process" is right up at the top of the list of responsibilities.

Bd responsibilities

The second thing is to be open about that requirement when you recruit new board members.

If adding "participation in the development process" to the list of requirements for board members turns people away – or prompts current board members to resign – that's one of the first signs of a gradual culture change.

While we lament the loss of board members, often people who resign when the rules change have simply been looking for a reason to leave.

As for those who say they don't want to be part of a board that requires participation in donor and fund development, that's also a dramatic sign you're changing the culture.

It's so much better to be clear at the outset about the culture you're creating, than to have to try to change people's performance once they're on board.

Respect the rituals of fundraising, even if you'd like to change them as quickly as possible.

In one organization I know, the corporate fundraising volunteer structure was one in which women were team captains and made no calls.

Appalled by the wasted potential of the women who weren't asking – many of whom were corporate executives themselves – the new development director sought to reorganize the program.

She met with fierce resistance – particularly from some of the women and from the man who was the program's lead volunteer. It took two years before all teams were integrated with men and women askers.

In this situation, the development director modeled the structure she wanted by setting up a separate major gifts program in which the chairs, team captains, and askers were men and women who shifted in and out of various roles easily.

Be a careful observer of the way things are celebrated – celebrations are a strong part of the culture.

In one of the many mergers that occurred in medical centers during the past decades, two foundations came together. They couldn't have been more different in nearly every respect of their culture, but it was in the way they celebrated that the contrast was most marked. This applied to both internal (staff) and external (board, donors, community) occasions.

The one, which was larger and more corporate, had done away with many of the small staff parties and celebrations years before, preferring more formal recognition through meetings, flowers, or lunches at local restaurants.

The smaller (but older) foundation had a family culture – potluck lunches, birthday celebrations at the office, and much more "down time" where they boosted each other through informal get-togethers.

It was the same for the recognition and celebration of large gifts and important donors. The one was much more corporate, the other more intimate.

In the end, the more corporate culture predominated and became the culture of the merged foundation.

If your fundraising culture centers on events, it may be difficult to reorient that same effort into developing a program of personal major giving.

In my first development director's job, the organization had nearly one event a month. Although responsibility for the events was shared by the board, specially recruited volunteers, and the auxiliaries, these events were time consuming and, with two or three exceptions, low revenue producers.

At the same time, the "major gifts" program was a "select mail" effort that asked for gifts of $100 or more.

Over the course of three years, we gradually trimmed and consolidated events, adding a second "blockbuster" that reduced the need for other smaller events, and, through a serendipitous challenge gift, brought the board's understanding of the power of the major ask into sharper focus.

Although the organization still has several events, it has now distinguished itself through both a major capital campaign and an endowment campaign.

Legends play a strong role in the culture of fundraising.

People love to tell the stories of those who, over the history of an organization, have been fearless askers, great event organizers, unexpectedly clever at finding the right way to solicit a resistant donor, or tenacious enough to keep asking even after hearing "no" five times!

Referred to as "war stories," people love to tell them and to hear them.

Listen carefully to these stories, because they encapsulate the culture. You'll find flashes of courage, creativity, and tenacity – and you'll build on the culture if you begin to recognize the new heroes and new legends each year. Add them to the list that already exists, and include them in the orientation for new board members.

Many of the legendary askers and organizers are either still involved or still available. Strengthen this special part of corporate culture by having them come back and tell their own story.

The way people prepare to ask for a gift – and the way they ask – is also indicative of the culture.

Some organizations are process oriented, requiring training, a buddy system of soliciting, and perhaps a term of service on the board before an individual becomes a full-fledged asker-advocate.

In other organizations, no preparation is suggested or encouraged beyond finding out who wants to ask whom, how well they know their prospects, what tools they need, and when they will do it.

Experience and the literature tell us that solicitations are more effective when there is *some* preparation. However, trying to force an effective asker into a training session will be counterproductive.

Carefully weigh the need for process when dealing with a culture in which Lone Ranger superstars are accustomed to going out and doing things on their own and with little preparation. If it's working, let them be. Train others who are willing, and gradually the culture will change.

Thanking is a ritual that's part of the culture.

Some organizational cultures are so strong on the thank-you process that they mishandle or over-control it. For example, if the person who is *supposed* to thank certain people is sick or unavailable, some organizations suspend the thank-you process until that individual returns.

Rather than follow this ill-advised approach, it's better to back up the ritual process with an official one that sends out the proper receipt or letter from the office, then circulates the list of those to be thanked to those whose traditional role has been to call, write, or send flowers.

In this way, the organization responds in a timely way, while still honoring the special touch that donors appreciate when the thank-you is highly personal and from someone they know.

In working with the culture of thanking in an organization, remember that systems liberate: if you install effective systems that back up the thanking rituals (personal notes, personal phone calls, thankathons), then you'll still be able to complete the process even if your ritual process occasionally breaks down.

In many organizations, the culture of fundraising minimizes the process of donor and fund development.

This may be the most important, and difficult, cultural aspect to alter. In organizations that have focused only on fundraising and not on the larger context of donor and fund development, soliciting is relegated to a few people. Others on the board or committees stand aside and let them do it.

In order to thrive, the most important cultural shift every organization must make is to create a culture in which development is understood and practiced by everyone – administration, program staff, development staff, board members, other volunteers – in all of its intricacies.

There must be a shift from a culture in which fundraising is compartmentalized to a single function – asking for money – to a culture in which development is an inclusive process in which everyone understands that all relationships have potential for enhancing the organization, and everyone plays a role.

Creating a culture of philanthropy requires an understanding of the entire development process.

Those who have been at it a long time know that fundraising is only successful when organizations focus on philanthropy – voluntary action for the public good as it relates to giving, asking, joining and serving — and when they follow that focus with development – the deliberate, authentic and intentional relationship building with current and prospective volunteers and donors.

In organizations where "development" is considered simply a euphemism for fundraising and not a separate and critical process, there's never the connection with donor-investors that leads to long term sustainability. It may sound strange but fundraising isn't about money, it's about relationships. And if you take the time to build relationships, the money will come.

Creating a culture of philanthropy also requires a respect for the culture that exists, and the aspects of it that need to be retained even as the culture evolves. Bob Waterman, in his book *The Renewal Factor*, discusses the importance of "surrendering the memories." At some point, change is blocked because we're fearful of letting go of what we do well – even if it's no longer what we should be doing. Waterman advises we need to learn to "take the best, and leave the rest."

Culture and values are tied together, and to address one without embracing the other will lead to friction and resistance.

•••

People who couldn't define their fundraising culture if asked, often reveal it in one simple statement – "We always...." Or "We never" or "We just don't think that would work here."

While you need to respect what you hear and see, and identify those parts that are so attached to the organization's values that they shouldn't be altered, still you'll want to evaluate the way in which the other parts of your culture can and should be modified or changed to accommodate your current vision.

5

Fundraising Communications

Early pundits in the development profession – people like Hank Rosso and Sy Seymour — rightly determined that fundraising is a marketing or exchange process. That truth has been with us practically since the beginning.

Because of this, the communications that support our development and fundraising activities are key. But due to time, personnel, or budget constraints, we often shortcut our communications efforts and diminish our results. Worse, we fail to assess the impact of our communications, frequently even missing the link between those communications and successful fundraising.

While it may be easy to track the connection between a powerful website and the number of online donations, it's more difficult to evaluate the short- and long-term impact of the other kinds of fundraising communications: letters, brochures, annual reports, proposals, thank you letters, requests for special support, even pledge reminders.

Objectivity may not come easily. Yet, to ensure that our messages are consistent, thematic, and effective, we need to ask ourselves the following questions:

• What do our fundraising communications say about our organization? What image do they convey?

• What messages are received by the readers of our letters and brochures or by the visitors to our website?

• When someone opens a direct mail or tailored request, what's their first thought?

• If we use telephone solicitations, how do our callers present our case?

• When was the last time we took a long look at our fundraising materials to evaluate their consistency, appearance, and potential impact? And,

• When was the last time we asked a group of people from the community – those who receive and hopefully respond to our communications – to give us candid feedback on what they're receiving?

We learn in every basic nonprofit course that a solid communications plan is the bedrock of successful fundraising. We're told it must precede, accompany, and follow-up all of our development programs – and all of that is true.

No matter which way we communicate – whether our messages are zooming through cyberspace or still delivered with a bulk mail stamp – there are some basic principles, discussed below, that still characterize effective fundraising communications.

First impressions are hard to undo: be sure that what people see or hear is what you want.

What's the first thing people think when they see your materials or website, or hear from a telephone solicitor? How do foundations and corporations react when they read your proposals? What's the first impression people have when they hear or read your message at a fundraising event?

If you're telling people about your impact, your results, the ways that you're meeting community needs and what a great investment opportunity your organization is for people who share your values, then you're on the right track.

If on the other hand you're conveying a message of desperation or urgent financial needs (even if you have them), then it'll be difficult to change this image even when things get better.

And remember – in any gathering, even with old friends and donors, there are people there who are hearing your message for the first time. It's always best to keep it focused on results.

While you're developing your materials, engage those close to you in honest feedback sessions

While market testing of messages is a given luxury of for-profit organizations, nonprofits seldom have the budget. It therefore becomes important to test your themes and messages among staff, board, and trusted donors before you put them out into the community.

One of the least expensive, yet most powerful, purchases you can make is a rubber stamp with the word "DRAFT" on it. Even if you're convinced your prose is stellar and your theme is powerful beyond criticism, have the courage to put DRAFT on the copy and circulate it to some people who'll give you candid feedback.

Do this with letters, case statements, annual reports, and any kind of communication where you only have one opportunity to make an impression. You want to make sure it's the best one.

Develop a theme for your communications that you'll use for a year or more, rather than changing the theme with each message.

Message resistance is acute in our culture. We're bombarded with messages from every corner, and have learned to ignore them. Researchers contend that it takes as many as seven messages before our resistance begins to erode.

So, if your goal is to build participation among your constituency, be sure every message has a consistent theme. The letters can vary in terms of the way the message is packaged, and your telephone callers can devise different ways of emphasizing the importance of every gift, but the core of the message over a significant period of time should be the same: your gift of any size counts – we want you to become an investor in our organization.

Fundraising communications should convey the community need you're addressing, not the need your organization has.

Talk about results, not needs. Talk about impact, not fundraising goals. Characterize the value of a gift not by the way it helps you meet your dollar objective, but by the way it changes lives.

While this may seem fundamental, there are still too many organizations focusing their letters, brochures, websites, and telephone solicitations on the importance of meeting their annual fund goal and the dire consequences for the organization if that goal isn't met.

Always keep your focus on the need you're addressing:

• Newsletters should profile your clients, playing down the board members with their wineglasses at the gala.

• Thank you letters should say how the gift is helping to meet the mission.

• Your website should carry a regularly updated story with pictures of how your organization is making a difference in the lives of the hungry, the homeless, youth leaders, or concert-goers.

And,

   • Telephone callers should be equipped with anecdotes that illustrate your work.

You don't need to spend a lot of money to have quality communications.

While those on a tight budget may sigh enviously over the four-color annual report from a local hospital or major university, there are ways to convey quality and substance without spending thousands of dollars.

In fact, organizations that have regularly produced glossy color-filled publications are now rethinking that practice in light of increased criticism from donors who feel it isn't a good use of their money.

There are two basic ways to cut costs and maintain quality. The first is to establish a relationship with a good graphic arts and printing company and ask them to produce your publications as part of their community philanthropy.

This worked superbly for the Djerassi Resident Artist Program in Woodside, California. Their annual report was itself a work of art, and done as a gift. The designer used the outcome as part of her portfolio, and Djerassi had a magnificent tool for its outreach and stewardship programs.

The second way to cut costs and maintain quality is to determine a "look" for all your communications that's classic and not dependent on gloss or color.

One organization did a magnificent series of fundraising communications in black and white, with screened photographs of exceptional quality and text that was powerful, succinct, and memorable. Over the years, people came to know and recognize (and respond to) the materials from this organization.

Evaluate the communications you're using, and make

changes in the way you get people's attention.

If we become too predictable with our mailings, if our website stays the same for months – or if we fail to package our message in a way that's different enough to capture attention – then we numb all but our most ardent supporters to our message.

Stand back from your communications and ask yourself how you can vary them just enough to maintain consistency while getting the intended market's attention.

Surprise your donors and friends by sending mail other than solicitations. San Francisco Shakespeare Festival sent a thank you Valentine to its donors. A dance company sent postcards to its donors while on tour. Executive directors often send along an article or white paper they know will be of interest. And a letter from a participant in your programs goes a long way toward convincing donors of the importance of their gifts.

Know the difference between development and fundraising communications.

Development communications are more like corporate institutional marketing: they convey the case without adding a "sell." They include annual reports, stewardship messages, public relations, and community relations.

Fundraising communications have a "sell" attached: they include remit devices, ways to give through your website, or the telephone solicitor's request.

Development communications are written and designed with the goal of building goodwill and a relationship; fundraising communications are intended to garner a response. The latter don't necessarily have a long shelf-life in the home or office of the recipient. They're acted on immediately, if at all. On the other hand, development communications may be kept, reviewed, and revisited by the recipient.

The goals of these two kinds of communications are related, but different. They'll also differ in tone and language. Development communications are written in a more narrative style and will sound and appear more institutional. Fundraising communications will use shorter sentences, more white space, bullet points, bolder images and active words.

Make time to develop powerful communications.

My secretary used to have a sign on her desk that said, "If it weren't for the last minute, nothing would get done around here." Unfortunately, that often applies to the year-end mailing, the annual report, or the proposal to a new foundation.

Remember that good communications lead to easier fundraising, and regular communications lead to easier renewals and greater reinvestments.

Put sufficient time into the preparation, production, and tracking of communications to ensure the best possible results. Use an action plan that spells out the steps in the process and assigns dates and responsibility for completion.

Few organizations have marketing directors – those that don't can engage volunteers (who are marketing directors elsewhere). While the production of the communications may fall heavily on staff, there are plenty of people in your community who would relish the idea of participating in a creative hour or two every several months.

Set aside professional time, as well, including an occasional day or half day for marketing, planning, evaluation, and idea development. It'll be more than worth the time.

Determine your communications goals before you begin developing your communications team or your materials.

Have an idea in mind about how you want to be perceived

before you ever work with volunteers or other professionals. While their input is essential and welcomed, if you're the professional then it's critical you know the outcomes you want before you begin.

Perhaps you've done a market survey and know that your visibility is low and the perception of your organization isn't exactly what you'd choose. For example, a community college may be viewed as traditional, essential, and respected – great descriptors all of them.

However, college administrators there may also want to be known as innovative, leading edge, and visionary. The college, in developing its marketing plan with the help of talented volunteers and professionals, will begin communicating messages to reach their long-term visibility goals.

If you're going to use the Internet for your fundraising communications, be sure to do so in a way that's appropriate for your organization, for the message, and for the potential donor.

There are two approaches to cyber fundraising: solicitations to your known constituency via email, and donations made via your website by people who may or may not know your organization.

The convenience of the Internet for fundraising needs to be balanced with the image of your organization, the content as well as the purpose of your message, and the preference of the potential (or renewing) donor.

Fundraising via the Internet has exploded in use and success, but it isn't for everyone or for every message. Test-market this medium among some of your long-term donors and gauge their reaction.

●●●

The printed word lingers, the spoken word flees, the Internet message may be filed or discarded without response. Knowing when to use each, and how to blend them into a powerful communications plan is one of the major factors in raising an organization's awareness in the community.

6

Integrating Your Marketing and Fundraising Messages

Does your 'to do' list look something like this:

• Get ready for year-end mailing
• Think about autumn appeal
• Prepare for annual report
• Review next year's development plan
• Create themes for community campaign
• Search for new ways to retrieve lapsed donors
• Consider ways of building a larger client base
• Explore options for more visibility
• Determine feasibility of partnerships

While these tasks may be daunting, they aren't unrelated. What ties them together – and can make any of them somewhat easier – is the opportunity to identify powerful marketing messages and weave them through everything you mail, propose, put on your website, or plaster on a billboard as part of your fundraising and general outreach.

The deliberate integration of fundraising and marketing is an activity too many organizations still neglect in spite of increasing evidence of its importance.

 Marketing and fundraising are so closely related because fundraising IS a marketing process: it is a values-exchange as much as an economic exchange.

People, perceiving the benefits of your work, invest something they value (their money) *in exchange for* the knowledge and evidence that you're advancing the things they value (child safety, education, programs for seniors, cultural and artistic opportunities).

Here is what's important to know about integrating your marketing themes and your fundraising materials into one powerful, compelling, and consistent message.

From the outset, fund development and marketing staff should work together.

Trouble comes to Divo. Cute

Too often, the will to integrate messages arises only after a crisis, or perceived confusion, or plans for a major new initiative.

A capital campaign often brings this issue to the fore. The intensity and timeline of a campaign serve as catalysts to staff and board, prompting them to focus more adroitly on a single message that will heighten visibility, increase donors, and take the organization to the new intended level. The need to economize and coordinate is strong, and the results can set the standards for the post-campaign era.

Rather than be at the mercy of external events, set a long-term plan for marketing and development coordination to position your organization to be more effective, visible, and successful for years to come.

Find a theme everyone agrees to, and stick to it.

It takes a lot of messages to get people's attention. Our problem is we expect dramatic results the first time we communicate our theme. But it can take years for the message to sink in, even if it initially attracts attention.

One national marketing director offered the observation that, by the time someone arrives at her office each day, she's already been bombarded with hundreds of verbal and written messages: billboards, radio, newspaper, family, road signs, television news, reports reviewed. Small wonder we have to be persistent.

A major university, deciding its theme would be increased alumni participation in the annual fund, stuck with that message for three years. It worked. Participation figures began to grow and now, with occasional reminders, are stabilized at a much higher percentage than before.

Focus on impact, not just product or reach.

Potential funders (and everyone else your organization would like to attract) are drawn to you because of your impact and how that meshes with what they value. If your issue is early childhood education, how many children are you reaching and what difference are you making? If it's seniors, how big is the need in the community for your programs and how are you meeting that need?

Starting a year-end appeal with "This year, thanks to people like you, 400 more seniors in our community know they're safe at night" is much more compelling than a letter that begins, "We are writing to ask your support for the annual campaign of Wentworth Village."

Keep it simple.

The simplest ideas are the most memorable. Clarify your most important message. If it isn't obvious, take some board and staff meeting time to distill the single-most important idea that conveys your mission. What is your greatest impact? What is the biggest benefit people get from your programming? What is the most important achievement you've made towards your mission? What dream are you beginning to realize?

One capital campaign for an assisted-living facility used that very phrase, "A dream is about to be realized" as its marketing theme. It was powerful, hopeful, and effective. Every proposal, every general marketing piece, carried the phrase.

Create a memorable tagline and use it on stationery, proposals, your website – everywhere!

"Transforming lives through education" is a strong statement a scholarship organization is using in its fundraising and general marketing.

"The tradition begins with you" was used by a start-up independent school in its student recruitment and fund development program.

"Because life is precious" is seen on the stationery and in development materials for a distinguished medical center.

Think about the jingles and slogans that have been burned indelibly into our minds via TV or radio – and try hard to create a memorable tagline for your organization. And, if you coin one, don't tamper with it. Let it become part of the philanthropic vocabulary of your community.

Test your marketing and development marketing ideas before rolling them out.

Sometimes, what we think will work in the community falls flat. Decades ago, there was the expression "run it up the flagpole and see if it waves." Old expression, good idea.

Convene a focus group, if only a casual one. Test your ideas in your newsletter with a request for feedback via email or phone. Use one of the relatively inexpensive survey forms now available on the Internet and ask key donors and volunteers to respond.

If you have some materials in print, circulate them with "DRAFT" stamped on them so people feel their opinion counts.

While it's tempting to present a new marketing and development marketing campaign in its entirety, you're likelier to have a winning theme – and engage people in its support – if you ask for their feedback.

Integrate more than messages: get your "look" to be one that is consistent.

Branding is a big deal in the for-profit and nonprofit sectors. Commit to typography (who doesn't recognize the typeface of Coca Cola?), colors (UPS brown is recognizable from close or far) and graphics that become uniquely your brand.

Scrutinize your logo – does it convey your impact? Is it interesting? Too many logos still look like the 1950s in the way they depict women or families or houses or elements of the community. Get yours up-to-date while also ensuring that all marketing pieces have a similar look. If you lay them on a table, side by side, they should connect.

Be sure to have a savvy marketer from your board serve on both your development and marketing committees to keep the coordination active.

See if one person will sit on both committees. Ideally, this individual would have marketing savvy *and* be someone who understands your organization.

If you can identify such a person, be sure he or she understands that their role is to advise, give feedback, and be the liaison from one committee to the other and to the board. It's not their job to run the marketing or development programs.

If you use a marketing consultant for general marketing, have that person look into your development marketing needs as well.

Most often, marketing consultants aren't trained in fundraising. But, once acquainted with the glaring similarities between marketing and fundraising, they often can see new ways to integrate values, benefits, and impact into all marketing opportunities.

Let them into your thinking, and you'll be encouraged by the way they enhance development marketing while fulfilling their general marketing charge.

When using an outside marketing consultant, remember that you have more expertise about the marketplace and development.

One organization engaged a capable marketing company to develop its logo, and then continued the contract by inviting the company to develop the initial fundraising materials.

The consultants developed a concept, and sample materials. No one who knew fund development liked it. Too many words. Flat colors. Redundant messages. Confusing graphics.

However, the consultants were so convinced they knew what was right that they budged only incrementally in subsequent meetings. The result? They lost the contract. The organization eventually generated its own words and images, integrating them more appropriately with the logo.

•••

Simplicity, power, and direction. These three words should characterize your overall marketing program as well as your development marketing program. To ensure the highest possible impact, be sure these two programs are integrated.

But, remember, while logos, themes, and design are important to your image and impact, they only add value when an organization has the other vital pieces in place: namely, a strong board, a compelling case, and talented staff.

No amount of fancy marketing can cover up major organizational voids. Be certain the infrastructure is in place – and then get out there in the marketplace with messages that tell your story in a single, powerful, and interesting voice. When you do, you'll watch your client base, friends, donors, and volunteers grow exponentially.

7

What You Should Always Communicate to Your Donors

We all know the importance of communicating with our donors. It is the basis of stewardship. It is how we create donor involvement and loyalty. But knowing *what* to communicate is as important as knowing *that* we need to communicate.

As donor expectations for transparency, accountability, and measurable impact increase, we find ourselves presented with new challenges and new opportunities.

Internet technology has increased our ability to communicate quickly and to tailor our messages to a specific portion of our constituency. The decreasing cost of reproducing videos and DVDs provides an inexpensive visual way to communicate our impact. And, increased involvement of well-coached volunteers adds a personal touch to our outreach to donors.

Whatever vehicles you choose, here are some things you should always communicate to your donors.

Whatever your message, frame it in gratitude.

You can never thank people enough. Preface every communication with continued gratitude for the donor's investment in your work. And make sure your appreciation is specific to the gift and its impact.

Also, try to tie it into the donor's personal motivation. "Your interest in our children's art program, which you've supported with generous gifts over the past five years, has made a huge difference in our ability to reach increasing numbers of children … We wanted to share with you a letter from a child in the 4th grade class at Longfellow School, one of the schools helped by your recent gift."

Reading that, or hearing it from a thank-you caller, the donor will have no doubt you know who she is and what her interests are.

Mirror the donor's values in your messages.

Remember that all philanthropy is motivated by values. People give to you because they share your values and it's important to continue mirroring these in your messages.

If the continuum of compassionate care is one of your key values, make sure you tell that story in your communications, with words and images. The patient with a nurturing doctor or nurse; the post-operative child surrounded by loving volunteers.

If independence for the elderly is at the heart of your mission, show your seniors in their homes with people helping them do things for themselves.

Reinforce your values through your messages, and your donors will be reminded of the values they share with you.

Convey progress towards a shared vision.

Along with shared values, shared vision is a major motivator for our investors. A program in New Orleans, created to reach children not served by Head Start, conveys its vision in this way: "Our vision is that every child in the greater New Orleans area will be ready when it is time to start school." The power of this vision is that it's about the community, not the organization. Furthermore, it is measurable.

If the baseline readiness percentage is (e.g.) 83 percent of children showing acceptable readiness, then you could communicate to your donors over time that the percentage of children who are ready is now up to (e.g.,) 85 or 89 or 93 percent.

The donor will feel like a participant in your success. More importantly, his or her vision of better prepared children entering school will be ignited again and will likely lead to further investment in your program.

Communicate good news, even if out of cycle with regular communications.

Don't hold off on good news until your regular newsletter. If something momentus happens, let your constituents know right away. A special award, early completion of a campaign, or simply a story letting people know good things are happening to the people you serve.

One organization communicated a breakthrough with a client – a runaway 13-year old who had successfully reunited with her family. The email described the joy of the family at having their daughter back, how the counselor they sent with the girl had helped reunite the family, and how grateful the organization was for the investor support that made such programs possible.

Communicate bad news, too.

While we're eager to communicate good news, we are reluctant to relay bad news. However, if we regard donors truly as investors – as part of our network of people who care about what we're doing in the community – then we'll also be willing to communicate bad news.

You didn't get the NEA grant. You didn't make the matching fund goal (or are in danger of not meeting it). Auditors have discovered a financial irregularity and you want to alert your investors before it becomes public knowledge.

Burying bad news is something we've seen too many corporations and nonprofits do in the past decade: be sure to share yours with key investors and volunteers. They'll be more willing to help if they're not surprised. Further, it makes them feel more important to be included in the early news, even if it's bad.

Let them know how they can help.

A donor's gift is a symbol of their trust in your ability to advance the vision and values they share with you. But, it's not the only thing they can offer. When communicating with investors, offer other opportunities for them to participate so they don't believe that all you're interested in is their money.

Ask if they'll participate in a focus group. Send them a survey and ask them to respond. Inquire whether they'd be willing to take a look at your new mission statement or case statement before it goes to print.

They may not be interested in helping, but if they are you'll be well-rewarded by the heightened sense of involvement they'll have. And, those who decline will still remember that you asked them.

Tell them how important they are.

Your donors are important to you, obviously. And, while all the above techniques will help them feel that way, sometimes it's good just to tell them how important they are. Directly.

"As a key supporter of our Home Help Program for the Elderly, you're very important to us. Each time we help an elderly person remain independent, we reflect on how important the support is that you and others provide. Quite simply, we couldn't do what we do without you, and we just wanted you to know. As one of our seniors at home wrote recently, 'You've given me the skills and support to stay at home, and my family and I can never thank you enough.' And we can never thank you enough."

Let them know how their support attracted the support of others.

Gifts leverage other gifts. I know from years of experience how big gifts attract other big gifts. But do we remember to let the majority of our donors – the aggregate of whose gifts make a huge difference for us – know that their support has attracted other support?

Foundations look at the breadth of support as well as the big gifts. Individual donors want to know that their large gift is supported on a platform of many smaller gifts.

Remember to let all your donors know that their gifts are magnets for additional gifts or for recognition by a corporate or foundation funder.

Be sure donors hear from a beneficiary of their giving at least once a year.

Generating a letter or email in-house is quick and relatively simple – and most often comes from a staff member. Be sure that your donors hear at least once a year from a beneficiary of your program.

The letter and drawing from a child, the phone call from the high school student, the video or DVD that captures the program in action and includes a voiceover from a recipient of the services, the appreciation from a dancer or an oboist or an actor for keeping the lights on and the audiences in their seats – all are memorable and have pronounced impact.

Investors measure the impact of their investment in many ways – but the anecdotal feedback from people who benefit directly is one of the most powerful.

Let donors know that they are your investors and stakeholders.

Although we convey this implicitly in many of our communications, we need to let donors know explicitly as well. It is parallel to the suggestion above of letting donors know how important they are.

Ultimately, your sustainability will be assured when donors move from viewing their giving as an annual transaction to viewing their investment as an ongoing opportunity to participate in your organization and in the transformation of your community.

When they think of themselves as investors, they view their responsibility, loyalty, and involvement in a different way.

Using investor related language (or "donor-investor" if that is better for your organization) opens communication doors that are limited when we think only of our investors as donors or contributors.

An investor relationship is dynamic; a donor or contributor relationship can be passive. Treat them like investors and stakeholders, and they'll be more apt to renew and increase their investment when asked.

•••

Communicating with donor-investors is essential. The new

65

philanthropists are curious, have high expectations of us, and are eager for involvement. They view their giving as social investment and, because they respond to the issues and values they care about, they expect to receive information that assures them their investment is well spent and having a significant impact.

Be sure your messages are not only appropriately frequent, but have content that will ensure long term donor-investor loyalty.

8

Understanding The Motivations of Major Donors

Motivated major donors. We want them, need them, strive to keep them. And yet, we find ourselves too often frustrated because we don't have them, still need them, or, worse, we've lost them.

Much has been written about major donor motivation. Sweeping generalizations profile the most likely big givers and so we find, in our communities, that we're all turning to the same people again and again.

Lists for feasibility studies contain the same names, year after year. In the back of performing arts programs, in annual reports and newsletters from social service organizations, and in the publications of independent schools and colleges, we see the same people. Over-solicited, these "most likely to be major donors" become increasingly resistant as donor fatigue sets in.

So, what's the answer? If the profile of the major-rated "Everydonor" is so proven, yet so exhausted, where do we turn to find the new major donor?

And, as important, how do we create the conditions in which even experienced donors will be more motivated and excited about the opportunities we offer them to invest in our communities?

Here, then, are the most important things to know about the motivations of major donors.

The old generalizations about motivation need to be rethought.

While recognition, peer pressure, the quest for immortality, and other traditional motivations still exist, it's important to realize that a younger generation of donors and the rising number of women in philanthropy have added new motivations that can prove beneficial to organizations that understand them.

Thirty-somethings and forty-somethings who have created the products and services that have made them wealthy are used to participating in the creation, implementation, and evaluation of projects. They respond to outcomes and want to be involved.

In some communities, the scions of wealthy families have departed from their philanthropic traditions and are directing money towards programs with high social impact rather than those with high social recognition.

It is the same with many emerging women donors. All the recent studies about women's philanthropy distinguish it from men's philanthropy with one common conclusion: women get involved first, and then give. They are less apt to respond to peer pressure; more apt to follow their own hearts.

Three basic motivations are connection, concern, capacity.

We focus on an individual's capacity, when we should first concentrate on their connection with and concern for the mission.

Too often, organizations think they can identify major donors by combing Forbes (for the 400), Fortune (for the 500), or their own local organizations for their lists of high-end donors. Those lists are an aid only if they bear names of people with a connection to your organization or who have shown an interest in your mission.

If someone is concerned about the issues you're addressing, then you can create the connection by building the relationship. Engage them in cultivation activities that are directed to their interests and issues and that connect them with like-minded people who share their values.

If the relationship (connection) already exists, but you're unsure about the issues and interests of the prospect or donor, you can engage the donor in events or meetings that strengthen the relationship while exposing him to the range of issues you address.

If the capacity to give is large, and the connection and concern are solid, it is a winning combination.

Motivation is an internal issue – what organizations provide is the right environment for that motivation to flourish.

One spin on motivation theory is that you cannot motivate people: they are already motivated. Your job is to find out what their motivation centers around and construct the right environment for it to flourish. With newer philanthropists, this is especially true.

When you've uncovered the connection and concern (see previous paragraph) you will have a much better idea about what motivates that donor.

Motivation grows out of values.

Something happens when you see a donor connect with the values, mission, and vision of your organization. It's as if there's an audible "click." Suddenly, the desires of your organization and those of the prospective donor are wedded.

The person realizes that this is the educational philosophy that will produce future citizens of which the community will be proud. Or this is the approach to programs for developmentally disabled adults that insures the most dignity. Or this is the dance company most closely reflecting the diversity he or she seeks in the arts and in the community.

When you hear that "click," know that your potential for engaging the donor for long term investment has increased significantly, and that your job now is to supply the information and experiences that will keep the motivation strong.

Motivation is ignited by the passion that comes from belief in the mission.

The age of the passive donor has ended. It died out late in the 20th Century, and I suspect it won't return. As the face of philanthropy changes, so does its quest. An interest in outcomes is replacing a need for rewards. While recognition is still important, the way in which it's provided is changing. It is more mission-connected.

Those who benefit, those who are served, those who are grateful for the programs and services: these are the individuals with whom thoughtful philanthropists want to be connected. It is they who fuel the passion that motivates continued giving.

Research may give clues about motivation, but the only truly reliable resource is the donor.

Make an effort to know as many of your donors – major or not – as you can. See them all as having the potential to give a large gift at some time or to connect you with those who can. If you're fortunate enough to have research capability at your organization, use it as a baseline.

But don't be lured by high-income zipcodes or indications of vast personal wealth unless you also know these individuals share your values and are concerned about your issues. Research is the starting point. But so much of if fails to tell us what we really need to know: what does this person care about? That's where conversation and involvement come in.

The goal of good stewardship is to keep the donor motivated.

Stewardship, which is the ongoing relationship with a donor based on mutual respect for both the source (donor-investor) and impact of the gift, is perhaps the most important function in the development process. It is critical to maintaining major donor motivation.

So many organizations lose major donors by failing to maintain a values and mission-based relationship. They wine, dine, and solicit prospects, only to forget about them once the gift is secured.

Just as we speak of donor-centered solicitations, we need to think about donor-centered follow-up and ongoing stewardship. Our traditional solicitation model is about us: we need the money, we find the prospect, we cultivate, we solicit, we get the gift and then thank the donor and put him into the file. How motivating is that? For staff, the transaction is over. But for the donor the relationship is just beginning.

The motivation of corporate and foundation funders is different from and similar to that of individuals.

71

Although corporations and foundations may be motivated by more complex factors in their giving (perception as corporate citizens, investing in a local or national agenda), they are nonetheless led by individuals.

When a corporation or foundation becomes a major donor, chances are it's because your organization matches the guidelines or fulfills the funder's commitment to a particular population, need, or ideal.

Most often, the process for obtaining a gift is relatively impersonal, requiring a certain level of objective application. However, during the gift-seeking process and afterwards, as stewardship is implemented, the motivations of decision-making individuals should be watched and responded to.

Motivated donors must be linked with motivated volunteers.

The increasing trend in universities, hospitals, and other larger organizations to use staff-only soliciting is unfortunate. The presence of a volunteer, motivated by the values and mission of the organization and giving of his time to meet with a potential donor, cannot be over-valued. The peer ask continues to be the most effective, and the most motivating, in major gifts programs.

This doesn't in any way undermine the training, effectiveness, or knowledge of development staff. Not at all. It's simply that the continued involvement of motivated volunteers - often with staff - in the cultivation and solicitation of major gifts produces the greatest results.

Ultimately, the most motivated major donors will self-solicit.

This concept, first introduced to me years ago by a motivated and effective volunteer at Stanford University, the late Bill

Kimball, has repeatedly proven true.

Self-solicit simply means that when we do a great job of connecting and cultivating and listening, the person we're engaging begins to think of ways he or she can become an investor in our organization. As the care and concern increases, the prospect begins to think of ways to make an investment – even before we ask.

While few donors will actually step forward without being asked, the self-solicit dynamic ensures that when the prospect is asked the ensuing transaction will be characterized by excitement, energy, and commitment.

It is the same with those who are already committed as major donors. They will renew and increase their gifts if a motivating environment surrounds them. The challenge to those who ask is to stay so connected to the prospect or donor that the right time to ask becomes obvious.

•••

Ultimately, the motivations of major donors are as varied as the donors themselves. Learn to look for the unique aspects of each current and potential donor: his values, interests, connections, and what he cares about. While some aspects of the traditional profiles still hold true, there's so much more to consider.

A broader view of motivation will bring a broader base of major donors, and among them will be the "new philanthropists" – those who are mercifully free of donor fatigue.

9

Keeping Your Prospect Pipeline Full

All organizations know the importance of keeping their pipeline filled with potential donors. What they often don't know is where to find the names.

We've all been to meetings where development committee or board members are pressed for the names of friends, neighbors, and colleagues. And there's probably not a person reading these words who hasn't been asked to review lists of donors from other organizations. This is particularly true during capital campaigns or just before an annual drive. People hit the panic button: where can we find more prospects?

But ongoing prospect identification is a key part of the three-prong responsibility of development officers and volunteers:

1) Soliciting and stewarding current donors,
2) Identifying and cultivating prospects, and
3) Maintaining the infrastructure to support our efforts.

Somehow, wedged between what many call "front-line fundraising" and the maintenance of staffing and systems to support the development program, the middle prong – identifying and cultivating prospects – often gets left behind until the shortage is felt. It's like running out of gas: if you wait until the warning light appears, and you have no source of fuel in sight, it's going to be a tough journey.

Here are important things to know about identifying prospective donors or spotting current donors who can be upgraded.

Analyze your own database before reviewing the lists of other organizations.

One performing arts organization, in its 10th successful season (but just beginning a formal individual giving program) was frustrated in its search for potential donors.

The organization gathered lists from similar arts organizations and board members carefully reviewed the names to see if anyone was familiar with the people or could make a secondary connection through a mutual friend. Additionally, they reviewed the business journals, newspapers, and other sources for potential names of people with wealth they could begin cultivating.

A consultant, called in to assist, asked how many people from their own subscriber and ticket buyer list were already donors and how many they had identified as good prospects. The response: it hadn't occurred to them to review their own subscriber and ticket buyer list as a source of prospects.

Yet when board and staff did this, the review yielded great results. Not only did the organization tap into an already-connected prospect list, it realized it had a large potential in the number of subscribers who were already giving but hadn't been formally solicited or properly acknowledged.

The result: the organization found itself with a long list of subscriber-prospects. It began serious stewardship of these people and launched a successful subscriber-giving program that continues to this day.

Not all prospects are prospects for first-time gifts: think, as well, of prospects for upgraded gifts who lie untended in your database.

The late Hank Rosso, founder of The Fund Raising School, taught his students that there are four types of donors: impulsive, habitual, thoughtful, and careful.

Impulsive donors are usually first time givers – they like your letter, your event, the article about you in the paper, or the person who calls and asks. They haven't yet thought deeply about the values involved or how they would fit in.

If these donors renew, the good news/bad news is they'll become *habitual* donors, giving year after year at the same level and telling their friends, "Yes, I always give $100 at Christmas to the Lung Association."

This can go on for years, unless effort is made to convert them into *thoughtful* donors: those who deliberate about their gift and peg it to the values the organization advances.

Finally, these thoughtful givers may make a *careful* gift – literally, a gift full of care. It can be a special, major, or planned gift, but it's often transformational in its impact on the donor and the organization.

Organizations that have a large number of habitual donors should consider creating an ad hoc committee to analyze the database and identify those who are stuck at a certain level. These names are reviewed, considered as a separate prospect list, and given special attention, stewardship, and outreach.

Most habitual givers haven't been truly connected to the organization's mission. The job of the ad hoc group is to make that connection.

Tend to big and small matters.

There's nothing random about developing a solid prospect

base. There may be windfalls – someone brings in an "A" list that you know will be a rich resource for you – but most of the fully functioning pipelines work because of careful attention to systems, both simple and a bit more complex

Take the simple. At all board, committee, and staff meetings, place a sheet of paper on top of the meeting packet that simply says, "Since our last meeting, I've met or thought of the following people who would be interested in our organization."

If each person provides just a few names each session, imagine how your list would grow. Using this approach (rather than, "Since our last meeting, I've met or thought of the following people who are well-to-do.") board members begin thinking of people with an interest in the issues and values of the organization, and they can begin envisioning how they might connect them to the organization.

Now, the more complex: When a critical mass (100 to 200) has been gathered, these names should be reviewed at a formal session described at length in another chapter.

If your organization has an active development committee, consider creating a subcommittee for prospect development.

As part of your systems and strategies, it's good to have one group in charge of prospect development. They gather the names that come in. They work with staff to "merge/purge" the new names against existing lists. And they create the lists that board, other volunteers, and staff will review.

Keep all prospect review sessions confidential.

There's nothing worse than having a prospect identification or review session turn into a gossip fest. This aspect of "prospecting" is one reason people balk at participating.

Set up your sessions so that lists are reviewed silently, and names are presented on easy to use forms.

While the narrative comments are always the most interesting, chances are your evaluators will be more apt to write comments if you've given them some boxes to check or multiple choices to circle.

When reviewers have finished, it's up to the prospect development committee to review, and discuss confidentially, the completed lists.

From this information, strategies for approaching prospects or upgrading donors are developed.

Keep the pipeline full of likely prospects – prune the deadwood regularly.

Lists aren't sacred. They should be culled, reviewed, cut, cleaned up on a regular basis. While in some situations there may be safety in numbers, the prospect pipeline isn't necessarily one of them.

Just like a New Year's resolution, pick a day every year when you print out the entire list, examine the activity reports, check against the returned mail reports, and look at the lapsed donors.

If you hate to lose anyone, then send out a special mailing asking people if they want to stay on your mailing list. Don't be afraid of the answer. Knowing that someone wants off your list is better prospect relations than keeping her on the list (and continually irritating her).

Find ways to identify new prospects for your pipeline.

Run a box in every newsletter (or provide your website URL) where you gather the names of people interested in learning more about your work. Do the same on your website, inviting people to recommend others to whom your mailed or emailed newsletter may be sent. At events, collect attendees' names through registration or through sign-in (if you have a good door prize, collect those business cards). They become part of your prospect pipeline.

In your newsletter or on the website, include a box readers can check indicating whether their name can be used when contacting the individual. If they say yes, send the first copy of your newsletter in an envelope and include a note such as, "At the suggestion of Gracie Martin, we are sending you this issue of our newsletter...."

If Gracie doesn't want her name used, send the newsletter in an envelope with a note from the executive director or board chair. It might say "It has come to our attention that you're interested in programs that address community needs similar to those we're involved with, and we're taking this opportunity to let you know more about our organization."

Use the same techniques to follow up with all names that come to you.

If you aren't sure whether you have enough prospects to reach your annual or capital goal, do a gift range chart early in the planning phase.

The gift range chart is one of the handiest tools in fundraising. By establishing the range of gifts needed to reach an annual or capital goal, the number of gifts at each step of the range, and the prospect-to-donor ratio at each level, you can get a pretty quick picture of whether you have enough prospects to reach your intended goal.

One organization, considering a capital campaign of $1.5 million was happily (and successfully) able to up its goal to $2.7 million when it did a detailed donor and prospect analysis.

The organization first developed a gift range chart for a $1.5 million campaign, but found that its own prospect and donor base, when formulated in the prospect-to-gift ratio, had much greater potential.

The converse can also be true. Many organizations have had to lower the goals of their annual campaigns when they began putting actual numbers of prospects against the needed gifts on a gift range chart.

Involve existing donors in prospect review and development.

Those who are already enthusiastic donors can be great sources of names of other potential donors. While we do this routinely with board members, remember to ask your other key donors as well. It extends their sense of involvement, and often they're willing to help cultivate and solicit the individuals they recommend.

Be sure the process of prospect identification, review, strategy development, and cultivation is characterized by confidentiality, sensitivity, and a values-inspired approach.

We're not looking for "pigeons" whose arms we're going to twist – this vocabulary is inappropriate even in the most confidential circles of your organization. Voluntary giving is a form of service to the community – it is the way people invest in and strengthen institutions that create excellent communities.

At every step of the way, development professionals and leadership volunteers need to convey the dignity of the process. From the way in which names are gathered, handled, and reviewed, through the cultivation and solicitation itself, you'll find many more people willing to help you identify prospects and upgrade donors if the process has integrity.

•••

The search for prospects needn't be a daunting activity if you create and implement systems and a structure to keep the process continually rolling – and if you remember that our sector provides untold benefits to its communities and its citizens. When you develop new names for potential involvement, you're laying the foundation for not only increased community impact, but for your donors personal fulfillment as well.

10

Cultivating Your Donors

It's no secret that a prime factor in successfully soliciting major donors is appropriate cultivation, which typically involves lunches, events, tours, and other timely and purposeful interactions between prospects and staff and volunteers.

But effective cultivation isn't random acts of kindness or even a series of unconnected activities. It is strategic, coordinated, and part of the overall solicitation plan for an initial or renewed gift.

The quality of your cultivation and follow-through has a major effect on the ease and success of the eventual solicitation. Here, then, are the most important things to know about the process of donor cultivation.

Cultivation is a partnership involving board members, volunteers, donors, and staff.

Staff choreographs and participates in opportunities for board members and other volunteers to meet and talk with prospective donors.

But volunteers must make themselves available for regularly planned cultivation events to which prospective donors will be invited. Volunteers should also be willing to initiate or participate in special cultivation activities planned with selected prospects who want more individualized opportunities to learn about the organization.

Current donor-investors are also important in cultivation. Their participation not only increases their engagement, it provides them opportunities to become advocates with your prospects.

Cultivation is strategic.

Although we tend to think of cultivation as parties and events during which we introduce potential donors to the people and mission of our organization, we should always think of cultivation strategically. Parties and events, without follow-up based on a cogent cultivation plan, are missed opportunities and lose their value.

Cultivation planning takes two forms: general and specific. Have a strategic plan for each. General cultivation is comprised of regularly scheduled events (e.g., first Wednesday tours and coffee; second Thursday program presentations) to which board and staff members bring people with interest in and potential for giving. Specific cultivation activities are those geared for special prospects, those who may or may not also attend regularly scheduled activities or events.

Both types of cultivation are geared to the interests of the prospective donor. Both require follow-through.

Cultivation is systematic.

After any kind of event or activity, a follow-through plan ensures a stronger connection with those who attended. Good techniques include adding the prospect names to your mailing list and thank-you letters that convey the success of the event or program.

An email or personal phone call from a board member or event committee member to patrons of the event also has considerable impact.

At cultivation or recognition events, assign a board member to each table (unless of course the table has been bought by someone for a group and is completely filled). Provide board members and other key volunteers with confidential lists and short biographies of those at their table (and make sure they leave that confidential information at home!).

Also, if some of those attending are part of your top prospect pool (or are already large donors), be sure a board member is assigned to look after those individuals.

Where tables are hosted, a member of the board or dinner committee can circulate graciously among the seated guests.

Cultivation should be coordinated.

All staff and volunteer interaction with prospective or current donors needs to be reported to the central coordinating officer of your organization – either the development director or, if there's no development department, the executive director or board chair.

There are several reasons for this. First, staff may have information that's critical to any conversation with the prospect (for example, previous gifts, previous outreach). Second, the prospect may be "on hold" for another opportunity or reason not known to the volunteers, and pursuing a gift at this time would be inappropriate. Third, the prospect may already have been assigned to another volunteer and the duplicate effort would send a confusing signal to the prospect. Finally, the volunteer (or staff person) may benefit from special information about the organization, for example, one of the organization's special projects that may relate to a prospect's particular concern.

An Action Update Form or other easily filled out, faxable form (or email connection) will make such coordination painless.

Cultivation shouldn't be limited to large gift prospects only.

During the year, include a cultivation component in the plans for every activity to which the community is invited. While this may seem obvious, countless organizations miss opportunities to showcase their impact to an unfamiliar audience.

Be sure that everyone who attends a gala event leaves the event with increased knowledge about your organization. Too often, people will comment about a great event but, when pressed for the organization sponsoring it, won't remember.

A brief presentation, materials at the table, a packet given to attendees as they exit the event: these will serve as tools for building a relationship with those not yet aware of or connected to your organization.

Not all cultivation involves personal interaction.

Simply providing information is another way to cultivate prospects. Your newsletter, whether sent by email or snail mail, is a form of cultivation, and can be used effectively for this purpose. But be sure it's communicating the message you most want your readers to receive.

• Does it convey the impact and results of your programs, or does it focus on your needs?

• Does it portray – in words and photographs – the kinds of people you're serving in your programs?

• Does it balance volunteer information, donor recognition, and program impact? Or does it overemphasize the social aspect of your organization and show, instead, too many photographs of your special events?

Newsletters are one form of non-personal cultivation, but there are others. Email is a marvelous cultivation and stewardship tool. It's quick, simple, and timely. If you have a program of known interest to a prospect, have the program staff person prepare a "white paper" relating your local program to an article in a magazine or newspaper that focuses on a local, national or international need your organization is addressing. Mail it or email it to interested donors and prospects (and include a thank you to the donor for helping to make the program possible).

A family service organization focused on its child abuse prevention program with a group of donors. An excellent article on the importance of prevention education was pulled from a major national newspaper. The position paper prepared by the staff person focused on what the local family service agency was doing to address this issue of national concern.

The article and the white paper were sent to prospects with a note emphasizing the importance of the local action in this area.

Cultivation, with or without systematic planning, can also occur unexpectedly.

Favorable press coverage of an event or program will heighten awareness among potential donors of your organization and its mission. Enthusiastic board members and other volunteers are often informal advocates, unwittingly arousing great interest among those with whom they interact socially and professionally.

The largest gift from an individual (nearly a half million dollars) to a social service agency I'm familiar with was made anonymously by an individual who became interested in the organization because of the enthusiasm and advocacy of one of its staff members.

The donor had no prior connection to the organization but, over time, respected the commitment of the staff member and shared the basic values and mission of the agency.

In another case, a bequest in excess of $1 million was received by a children's services agency from a woman whose only experience with the organization was through a neighbor who was a dedicated volunteer and would share stories of her experiences with her friend.

Both of these gifts were the result of a relationship with an individual who was committed to an organization, but were not part of a deliberate cultivation plan.

While it's important to cultivate, know when to ask.

The quality of your cultivation and follow-through has a major effect on the ease and success of the eventual solicitation. Those responsible for monitoring the cultivation of key prospects must recognize signs that a prospect is getting close to where she can be asked for a gift. Use your intuition when cultivating: it will send you valid signals.

Cultivation, because it is pleasant and painless, can easily become a consuming activity. But continuing cultivation staves off the inevitable: asking for a gift. You must watch the prospect for signs of growing interest and willingness to be involved. If she's asking, "How can I help?" or "What can I do for this project?" or "Is it possible to get more involved?", then you have done a great job.

Cultivation of corporations and foundations is different from cultivation of individuals in one major respect.

With a corporation or foundation, you usually know before the cultivation begins what the deadline is for a funding request and what the process is for closing the gift. It's easier to sequence the activities and organize the involvement of the corporate or foundation representative in a way that matches this timeframe.

With individuals, there usually isn't such a calendar (except for every organization's push for year-end tax-motivated gifts). Beyond that, the same rules apply: cultivation must be systematic, coordinated, and strategic.

Be sure there's a budget for cultivation.

Not every development expense – and cultivation is a prime example – has a predictable or immediate return.

As a result, it isn't always easy to convince treasurers or controllers that cultivation activities are a necessary step towards gifts that may be realized months or even years later.

It's critical that your cultivation and stewardship activities be part of your budget and funded adequately. Otherwise, you won't be able to sustain your cultivation program. And, if you don't, there will be a negative effect on your capacity to raise funds.

It helps make the case for funding cultivation if development officers keep stories and anecdotes handy about prospects who became significant donors because they had appropriate cultivation and stewardship.

•••

Cultivation is both a process and a tool. Its counterpart, stewardship, occurs after the gift has been made. Both activities are characterized by a focus on the donor, opportunities to learn more about the organization, a high degree of coordination, strategic thinking and planning, and excellent follow-through.

11

Peer Screening and Rating

Few things we do in fundraising are more sensitive or require more discretion than peer screening and rating. In whatever way the process is conducted, ethical issues and confidentiality are primary concerns.

The most common approach is one where board, staff, and volunteers meet to review, discuss, and rate a prepared list of potential donors.

In these sessions, lists of names are distributed and discussed, name by name, the primary aim being to identify the top prospects. Sessions like these – some of which become too personal – are both fascinating and uncomfortable: curiosity and aversion mingle, and people both hate and love the process.

Silent prospecting – in which screeners *write* their comments and discussion (and gossip) is avoided – is the more comfortable process for many. People will often take hours to review a long list, noting the interest areas of potential prospects, and providing information on as many as 200 names at a time. When silent prospecting is used, the "rating" part of the process is conducted in a follow up meeting, once the comments and rating suggestions of the screeners have been collated, analyzed and summarized. (For more on silent prospecting, see my book,

Beyond Fundraising, Chapter 4.)

Whatever screening and rating method you use, here is what's important to know to help ensure you stay within the boundaries of taste, ethics, and productivity.

Prepare the lists carefully.

Establish a "pipeline" program that keeps names rolling into the development office on a regular basis. Don't quash enthusiasm for turning in names by requiring full addresses or too many details – often the name of the town or the street is sufficient and you can research the rest.

Many are reluctant to submit names because they're not sure of the process for reviewing: they fear their name will be used without permission or those they recommend will be solicited prematurely.

Let people know there is integrity to the process, and practice confidentiality from the outset. The more people are comfortable with the process – from name gathering to actual solicitation – the more apt they'll be to keep the pipeline filled with potential donors.

Choose the screeners well.

When setting up peer screening and rating meetings, invite people who will respect the process, do the job, and have something to offer regarding the list of names.

Affinity groupings work well: in one church-related campaign, excellent results in screening were obtained by gathering groups of parishioners, members of Diocesan councils, people from the wider community, and those representing a retirement home connected with the organization. They each reviewed lists related to their affiliation with the church.

The number of names screened in that process was much

higher than if all people connected with the church had been given the same list.

This process works well for capital campaign screening.

Keep the discussion to what is important, not what is interesting.

The head of prospect research at a major U.S. university once told me that the hardest part of supervising his researchers was to convince them to focus on what was important, not on what was interesting.

When coaching the screeners, let them know what you're looking for. Structure the forms around connection (who do they know), concern (what are the interests of these people) and capacity (what do they know about the prospect's overall giving in the community).

Don't waste the time of those agreeing to screen.

Few things are more irritating to busy people than attending a poorly organized or ineptly run meeting. Be sure each person has the appropriate list, and that forms are neatly prepared with the name and address of the prospect.

Begin promptly when people arrive, and let them leave when they're finished. See that the instructions are clear, and that latecomers can read what they're supposed to do without feeling as though they're disrupting.

Keep the meeting moving and don't let the conversation drift into gossip or speculation.

Consider doing silent prospecting before conducting a rating session.

It's a good idea to separate prospecting and rating.

Engage as many people as you can in silent prospecting sessions. Then take the results of these reviews and analyze them. See where there's consensus. Identify the most highly or frequently rated prospects.

Then prepare a shorter list, with information taken from the screening session, and rate it with a smaller Prospect Review Committee (making sure this committee is representative of your constituencies).

In my experience, this process is more effective by far.

Be sure people understand the purpose of the session.

Electronic screening of your data base may yield top prospects according to zip code or various sorts, but the importance of hearing from people who actually know the potential donors is critical.

Be sure people understand the entire process: identification, qualification, development of strategy, cultivation, assignment, and then and only then solicitation. These sessions can be a very effective way of educating people about a dignified and sensitive development process.

Let participants know the value of their input by sharing successful solicitation results with them.

If you combine a well-handled process with good results (money in the door), you'll have willing participants in your future screening and rating sessions.

Letting participants know when a gift is received, even if that person wasn't involved in the solicitation, is important. If these individuals are known to the screener through church or some other affiliation, it's a wonderful gesture to be able to personally thank the donor for his gift.

Conduct sessions quarterly, whether in campaign mode or not, so that no one session has too many names to review.

It's easy to think "screening and rating" when a capital or major gifts campaign is looming. Ah, but how smart the organizations are that do these sessions on a regular basis. They're the ones whose prospect lists are ready to go when they are.

Build screening and rating sessions into your ongoing development program. By working to keep the pipeline full, it's possible to have 50 to 100 names to screen every quarter. Staff and key development volunteers can then work with these names and begin formulating the key lists well ahead of the campaign.

Offer participants something to eat and drink, a convenient time and location – and perhaps something to stimulate their minds.

Several organizations I've worked with – ranging from environmental to social service to educational – have combined prospecting sessions with a meeting or lecture. Whether or not you choose this approach, be sure to offer people something to eat or drink. One organization, wishing to maximize the number of people who could participate in their prospecting program, arranged to have four session options: one over breakfast, one over lunch, and two at the end of the day. People were able to choose which time was best for them.

Emphasize the confidentiality and discretion you expect, and model it yourself.

Remember, participants will be looking to you for their cues. It's important to model the kind of confidentiality you want them to maintain. Never make inappropriate jokes, asides, or comments. Before you say or write anything, ask yourself: "Is this something that I'd be embarrassed to have the prospect see or hear?"

•••

The refinement of prospect research is significantly advanced by good peer screening and rating sessions. For maximum effectiveness, be mindful of the integrity of the process, the need for discretion and confidentiality, and the importance of letting participants know how their participation advances your ability to raise money.

While peer screening and rating sessions are the way we prioritize lists of prospects and gain meaningful insights into their interests, capacity, and linkages, remember there is another step that follows: getting to know the prospect! Only then will you have true validation.

12

What Really Motivates
A Board to Raise Money

Just when I thought I had it figured out – that board members will go out and raise money when they "get it" about mission, vision, and values – and have confidence in their own ability to ask – I found that wasn't enough.

I observed that board members and non-board volunteers, even in organizations with a well-expressed mission and vision, are still reluctant to raise money, despite abundant training and confidence-building sessions.

Because much of my time is spent working with boards in this area, I was puzzled. More and more I wanted to know what the "tipping point" is: why some boards get out there and do it, and others, no matter how well-versed in the case and trained, still won't. So, I listened, observed, and asked questions. It didn't take long to sort out some conclusions that I pass along as things you should know about what *really* motivates your board to ask for money.

Clarity about the message.

Board members need to be clear about the marketing and

development message of your organization. Even if well trained in the asking process, lack of clarity will keep a volunteer from properly presenting your case to potential donors.

All volunteers (board and non-board) need a single clear and compelling statement that summarizes why your organization merits support.

"Messaging" (as the marketing folks call this process) is the new focal point for many organizations. Why you exist, what you've accomplished, how the community has benefited, and why your organization is a solid investment with a high return for the donor-investor – how clear are your messages?

Specificity.

Don't be vague about what you want the board member to do. In particular, be specific about timelines, deadlines, and strategy.

The leaders or professionals overseeing the development process should lay out the workplan for each board member. Give assignments. Be precise about contact information, possible approaches, cultivation opportunities, the deadline for asking, and the deadline for closing.

Specific assignments with clear instructions and end dates usually motivate board members. This approach is also easier on those managing the campaign. They know each volunteer's assignments and have specific talking points to follow when nudging them about deadlines.

Expectations.

Closely tied to clarity and specificity, expectations are also critical to motivation. Joe Batten, author of *Tough Minded Leadership*, reminds us that we're always judging people based on our expectations of them – but seldom do we remember to express those expectations openly.

When you give an assignment, convey *how* you'd like it to be carried out (such as, "Bring the person to a particular event, arrange for a lunch meeting with the CEO, take the person to the site, involve another person in the solicitation").

When conveying these expectations, ask for the person's agreement that this is how the assignment will play out – or, if they want to do it another way, discuss it with them. When people know what's expected of them, they're more apt to fulfill their assignments.

Appreciation.

For most people, fundraising isn't easy. It takes a lot of preparation and a dose of courage even for the most confident askers.

Appreciating board members and non-board volunteers is always important, but it's imperative now. And not only for the person who raises lots of money, but also for those who build relationships that will produce a larger base of donor-investors down the line.

Walking the talk.

Illustrate the mission, vision, and values in what you do and say. It's one thing to have written information in the volunteer training materials, it is something altogether different to connect board members and volunteers with the mission by giving them regular dosages of tours, testimonials, and personal meetings.

If words have no passion of experience behind them, they're just words. They won't keep volunteers buoyed through successive solicitations.

Minimal disconnects.

When you send board members and other volunteers out to ask for money for a specific campaign, be sure you have your numbers in place and your commitment is firm.

Nothing is more discouraging to volunteers than the disconnects that occur when financial or program goals change or when campaign totals and deadlines become moving targets.

Board members and other volunteers are community representatives. Don't put them in a situation where goals expand and contract, or, worse yet, where solicited funds have to be returned because the project failed to materialize.

Effective staff support.

Board members stay motivated in direct proportion to the efficiency and professionalism of the staff supporting their work. Wrong or late information, poorly researched prospects, cancelled appointments, inappropriate pressure, criticism, or spotty support will undermine even the most enthusiastic board member.

While a few stalwarts will make their calls despite poor support, most will not. To keep volunteer satisfaction high, don't make more assignments than your staff leadership can oversee.

Curtailment of conflict.

If various board members or volunteers have issues with your organization (its operations, structure, or fundraising goals) deal with these issues outside of board meetings if at all possible.

Conflict at meetings is detrimental to motivation, and the seeds of dissent can flourish into a harvest of discouragement and discontent. Aside from the awkwardness of such moments, otherwise enthusiastic volunteers will begin to question the organization and may lose interest or – worse yet – convey their uncertainty to others.

There's nothing wrong with healthy dissent, but a process for handling it outside of board meetings is a sound idea.

Clear understanding of the board and staff roles in fundraising.

Volunteers perform better when they know how their job relates to that of the staff person, and staff people work well with volunteers who respect their professional responsibilities.

While some volunteers continue to hope that the presence of a development staff will relieve them entirely of the job of fundraising, most realize that the development staff's role is to support the board in its fundraising and to be partner and teammate.

Mastery of mission, vision, values.

Every so often, it's necessary to revisit the mission (why you exist) or the vision (what your organization wants to do and what the community will become if you're successful) or your values (the shared beliefs that motivate you and get community members involved) – before you can get on task.

Set aside time at a board meeting or retreat, particularly if you're embarking on a new campaign or initiative, and reflect on these three critical aspects of your organization.

Doing so will not only help you recapture energy, passion and excitement, it will help infuse your board members with increased motivation to go out and ask for money.

•••

Getting and keeping board and non-board volunteers motivated about fundraising is both a discipline and an art. It's as much about organizational skills as it is about inspiration.

With today's demanding philanthropic climate, and the pressures facing people in their daily lives, it's more important than ever to treasure your volunteers and support their motivation. You can be sure your fundraising will flourish as a result.

13

Getting Your Board to Make Personal Solicitations

Fundraising is a contact sport. There's no doubt about it. In-person asks by peers of the would-be donor bring larger investments than letters, phone calls, or requests from a staff person. No special or major gifts program can succeed without face-to-face solicitation.

As proven as this principle is, the process of helping most board members take a leadership role in personal solicitations can be a challenge. The reasons for reluctance are commonly known: fear of rejection, lack of comfort with the entire concept of asking for money, a feeling of begging, and – if there's professional development staff in place – the belief that having such a person in place relieves board members of having to raise money.

Most experienced board members know they should be involved. They've been told (repeatedly) that part of their board member role is the personal solicitation of larger gifts. Heads nodding in agreement at the campaign kickoff (where spirits and enthusiasm run strong), they will set ambitious goals and vow to take at least five individuals to breakfast or lunch.

When the new day dawns, however, their old doubts and uncertainties return. Assignment cards are set aside until the deadline approaches, at which point a hurried phone call or a letter substitutes for the requested personal meeting. The effectiveness of the ask is diminished, and the response is very often disappointing.

The gulf between the acceptance of the theory (that the best solicitations for major gifts are personal asks) and the enthusiastic participation by board members in the solicitation process is often vast.

Bridging this gulf takes patience, understanding of the source of the reluctance, solid training and coaching of volunteers, and perseverance. It may take months or years to raise the comfort level of some board members to where they can participate. For others, it may never be possible. It's important to let these individuals know the roles they can play in the larger process of development.

Here's what to do to get your board members more involved in the personal solicitation process.

Solicit your board members first, and personally.

Far too many organizations solicit their board members by mail, telephone, or "group ask" at a board meeting. Then, they expect these same board members to make face-to-face solicitations from others in the community. But if they're not asked personally, how will they know how to approach others? And, why will they perceive it's important to arrange a face-to-face meeting?

It is much more effective as a training and coaching tool – and as a way to get to know your board members better – for the CEO and the Board Chair to solicit each board member personally during the year.

Objections to this process are often strong: board and staff leaders cite lack of time, and the idea that board members needn't be solicited personally since they're "part of the family."

But the time spent in that one hour (or less), listening to their concerns and enthusiasm, is critical to deepening the board member's involvement and it's a modeling exercise in how to ask for a gift face-to-face.

Be sure all board members have been asked to give before they're asked to solicit.

This principle is so proven it doesn't require much discussion. Believe it. Because inclusive language (for example, "join with us," "be part of this vital program") is such a critical part of a successful solicitation, it's critical that all board members who ask for gifts can, with authenticity, say "join me." It's also important that board members are able to say with comfort, "Our entire board is supporting the organization and its work."

Involve board members in the development process before requiring them to raise money.

Too many personal solicitation programs neglect the importance of the development process. Succumbing to the widely-held notion that "development" is just a nice way of saying "fundraising," they overlook the importance – to the donor and the asker – of the steps that precede the ask.

The planning and organization of a major gifts program should involve six steps prior to solicitation: identify/qualify, develop initial strategy, cultivate, involve, evaluate, assign. Then the prospect should be personally solicited.

Afterwards, there are three more steps in which board members can become involved: follow-through and acknowledging, stewardship of the gift and the giver, and renewal.

When board members get involved in the first six steps, they're much more apt to want to be involved in the seventh. And, when they're also involved in the last three steps, they begin to see the cycle and flow of development, not just the one-shot act of fundraising. And their comfort level rises.

Emphasize the importance of developing donor relationships.

When organizations engage boards not just in "fund development" but in "donor development," the focus shifts appropriately from the organization to the donor. The entire language of development and fundraising becomes donor-centered, and the needs and interests of prospective or renewing donors become the framework of the solicitation.

Fear and cynicism decline, and phrases like "arm twisting," "hitting someone up" (or other regrettable descriptions of the invitation to invest in an organization) disappear. And, with their disappearance, much of the apprehension about fundraising wanes.

In solicitations, board members hear the donor's needs and concerns, rather than focusing on their own worries. They share their enthusiasm about the organization's impact and results, rather than laboring over the organization's financial needs.

The act of asking becomes not one of pressure, but of release, as the donor and the asker forge an investment strategy to accomplish mutual goals in the community through the efforts of an established or proposed organization.

Train and coach.

Offer formal training – attended by all board members whether they'll be askers or not – as part of the preparation for the personal solicitation program. A balanced training session will include elements that inspire, motivate, and inform. Case histories or personal testimonials from those who have participated in or benefited from the program inspire volunteer solicitors and give heart to the appeal.

Motivation to ask is increased by presenting compelling documentation of the need the organization is meeting, observable impact of the programs, and the importance of increasing its outreach and service.

Adding a personal solicitation role-play also helps.

In addition to formal training, volunteers will need an assortment of aids. Written materials, videos, explanations of programs, answers to the most likely objections: all of these form the "tool box" that helps board members build their confidence to interact with a potential donor.

Also, equip solicitors with the information about the prospect they'll need to make a well-placed ask. They should know the person's giving history, their interests and involvement, and what other organizations they are involved with. Remember to convey only information that is public knowledge.

Emphasize the importance of being themselves in a solicitation.

While masterful solicitors have some traits in common, many of which can be acquired through the steps outlined above, a major value in having broad involvement in the asking process is the delight of seeing so many different and natural styles.

Donors dislike "slick" askers. The whole rationale for a peer solicitation is that the person being asked feels comfortable with the person asking. Encourage board members to be themselves, while striving to demonstrate the qualities of effective askers: well-prepared, while not appearing rehearsed; excellent listener; able to handle objections; willing to admit they don't have an answer; enthusiastic; focused on the purpose of the meeting;

and comfortable with the process of asking.

Team every board member with another board member or staff person for the call.

Pair an experienced board member or knowledgeable staff member with a board member who's just getting comfortable with the process (or with the organization).

Team solicitations are more effective than one-on-one asks, and they also raise the comfort level of the less experienced asker. And, many donors report that a team of individuals with whom they can converse and interact is more comfortable than a one-on-one meeting which may become awkward if conversation lags.

Team solicitations should be well-planned before the meeting to avoid confusion over which person carries which portion of the solicitation. Also, it's a good idea to let the prospect know that two or more people will be coming, and to explain who each person is and why he or she will be present.

As a staff person, be willing to play a key role in setting up the appointment and preparing the board member for success.

This is a team effort, and often the primary role of the staff person is before or after the ask.

The development officer will be involved in: setting up the appointment ("I'm calling at the request of ... to ask when it would be convenient for ... to meet with ... to discuss ..."), preparing prospect profiles, sending out a "pre-solicitation" letter or packet, providing follow-up information, and acknowledgement.

To further enhance the comfort and success of the board member, the staff person should offer one-on-one coaching before the meeting, thorough review of the case and the information on the prospect, and a review of the possible objections the asker might hear and how to respond. It is best, of course, if the staff person accompanies the board member on the call, but the preparation described should take place whether or not the staff member is going with the board member.

The partnership between board and staff – and the feeling of mutual trust and respect – is vital to raising board member comfort with the solicitation process.

Shed old attitudes about fundraising throughout the organization and bring board members closer to the program and its results.

All fundraising requires a deliberate retirement of the "tin cup" attitude that guided far too many nonprofits for decades. It was based on the idea that nonprofits were "needy" organizations.

The principle which should guide nonprofit asking – and help relieve some of the objections and anxiety of board members and other volunteers – is this: nonprofits require community support because they *meet* needs, not because they *have* needs.

This shift in attitude removes one of the biggest obstacles to asking, the fear of being perceived as a beggar. When this attitude can be conveyed, askers find themselves focusing on results, not needs. They can speak comfortably and enthusiastically about the impact the organization is having in the community.

This requires much more interaction between the board and program staff. Some of the administrative filters may have to be removed so that program staff can communicate directly with board members about their program results and funding opportunities.

Make sure each board meeting reinforces program

results, the value of board member involvement in development and fundraising, and has time set aside for appreciation of efforts.

Getting board members involved in the personal solicitation of major gifts requires a cultural change in some organizations. It means identifying the link between successful asks and program strength, and recognizing the efforts made by board members to get out in the community and advocate for the organization.

Keep board members close to the "product" by including a program presentation (not a report) at all board meetings. And, be sure to celebrate even small wins. In one national campaign, volunteers were reluctant to get started with their calls for all the reasons recited above. Motivation and results increased dramatically when the organization – drawing on a theme that had been developed in the volunteer training program – began sending out certificates to those who made their first personal face-to-face calls.

Whimsical, informal, and highly prized, these certificates identified those recipients who had "earned their spurs" by making their first call. As a motivation tool, it worked.

•••

The only failure in fundraising is not asking. The personal meeting opens the prospect's mind and heart to your organization and, even if a gift isn't made at that time, the process opens the door to establish and maintain communication. At some later time, a gift may be forthcoming.

Still, if the board member can't overcome his reluctance to ask, don't force the issue. There are plenty of important steps in donor development on which the individual can focus.

14

The Dynamics of a Solicitation Call

The time has come. You know it's right. All signs point to it. Your prospect is ready to be asked.

Getting to this point has taken time, cultivation, probably a few "test conversations" about becoming a donor, and a great deal of listening and waiting for the right opportunity. So far, so good. Now, you want to make sure the solicitation call goes well.

The right dynamics will ensure that your prospect's experience is positive, and that the desired transformation – from interested prospect to excited donor – takes place.

The key thing to remember is the paradoxical nature of the solicitation call. For the organization seeking the investment, it's the culmination of the process. But for the prospective donor, it's the beginning or the renewal of a long-term relationship. At least it should be.

If it is viewed by the organization as the long-anticipated end point ("We got the gift at last!"), rather than the beginning of a deeper relationship ("We see so many ways we can involve the person further."), then chances are that's what it will be.

And, if the organization returns to that same individual a year later, hoping for a similar investment, it may be disappointed. Remember that giving is transformational, not just transactional. I'll focus here on the more transactional side of the process, but its undergirding is deeply attached to the transformational nature of giving. Giving transforms prospects into donors and then, depending on the impact of the gift, transforms programs, institutions, individuals, and entire communities.

To lose sight of the transformational nature of giving is to let go of the values basis of all philanthropy, development, and fundraising.

Here's what you need to do to ensure that the solicitation call is donor-focused, values-based, and well executed.

Be certain the timing is right.

Watch for signals from the prospect: deepening interest, probing questions, greater involvement, and the willingness to comment and counsel on your programs and projects.

Hear your prospects when they speak of their own personal circumstances (recently-sold business or home, an inheritance they want to do something with, appreciated property, the last child graduating from college). They may be offering clues that the time is right to make a major current or planned investment in your organization.

Life, as has been said, is all a matter of timing. It is true for solicitations as well.

Be prepared.

The Boy Scouts' motto is a good one for nonprofit volunteers and managers –particularly when it comes to the dynamics of the solicitation call. There's no substitute for good preparation.

The introduction of "moves management" strategies by David Dunlop of Cornell University has made good managers and their volunteers more conscious of the natural flow of the solicitation process. A good solicitation call is an outcome of intense preparation, cultivation, planning, testing, and research. On the timeline of development, it is the smallest step. But, on the register of importance, all the other steps can be meaningless without it.

A sage once said there are four things you must do to be successful in any endeavor: plan, plan, plan, and do. Of course, you can over-plan and miss the opportunity to ask at the right time – but most problems in solicitations come from lack of planning, not too much planning!

Be ready ... for the unexpected.

It's one thing to be prepared for a meeting. It's quite another to be prepared for the unexpected.

Once, in a brand-new job for a university in the middle of a capital campaign, I had spent several of my first days on the road making calls with the chair of alumni major gifts.

As we were winding down our travels, preparing our contact reports in my office, I had a call from the vice president inquiring about the status of a match we were trying to raise for an NEH challenge. I reported that we were about $65,000 short, but I had some prospects in mind.

When I got off the phone, the volunteer asked me about the challenge. He then revealed that he'd never been asked for his gift and that, although he and his wife had thought of giving $50,000 he would like to close the NEH challenge with a gift of $65,000.

Was I prepared? No. Did I do what I had to do? Yes. Were the lessons great? You bet.

In another situation, I had carefully planned a call, worked out an elaborate choreography for when I would ask, and concerned myself with the other details a manager or volunteer worries about when imagining how the meeting will go.

A volunteer and I waited for the prospect, going over last-minute strategies. But the prospect had another scenario in mind. He walked in, sat down, and said, "OK, how much do you want?"

We sputtered and tried to delay the answer, but he was insistent. Knowing the importance of a donor-centered meeting, we told him. He smiled and said, "Now, tell me what you were going to tell me. I'm not a good listener when I don't know what the question will be!"

In both cases, a gift was made – but the biggest gift was an insight into the importance of being prepared for the unexpected!

Be informed.

For the dynamics of the call to work well, you must be as informed as possible about your organization, the project, the prospect, the way in which a gift can be made - and be current on changing circumstances with the prospect.

You don't often get a second chance to ask. You may come back to discuss the request, you may bring more information, but that kind of follow up is the natural outcome of a well-structured call.

Most calls that go awry do so because the solicitors haven't done their homework, are unable to answer tough questions or handle objections, make an inappropriate ask, or fail to be donor-focused in the conversation.

Be confident.

There's no substitute for confidence when soliciting a

prospect. And there are several aspects to this confidence.

First, have confidence in yourself as a representative of the organization and its mission. Get trained, even if you feel you know how to ask. This will reinforce what you already know and further boost your confidence.

Second, have confidence in your organization. If you're not a believer, how will you convey the importance of investing to another? Be familiar with its strengths, and willing to discuss its shortcomings. There's no need to be defensive. No organization is perfect, and the willingness to discuss strategies for helping the organization shows you are an informed volunteer.

Third, have confidence in the nonprofit sector as the vehicle through which donors build their communities. Speak confidently of the impact an individual's gift will have not just on the organization, but on the overall betterment of the community (seniors helped, teens counseled, animals protected).

Be enthusiastic.

Nothing is as off-putting to the person you're meeting with as lack of enthusiasm.

Enthusiasm doesn't have to be boisterous or inappropriate. It can be quiet, constant, and signaled by the twinkle in your eye when you speak about the impact of your organization in the community, or by the catch in your voice when you tell the story of one life changed by your programs.

Years ago, sales people for CUTCO Cutlery would make door-to-door calls to sell their top-of-the-line knives. When the sales people were trained, and given their satchels of knives to sell, the sales trainer would ask them, "What sells CUTCO?"

And they would have to answer, in unison and in very large voices, "Enthusiasm!" It is the same with us. If we are enthusiastic, others will be. Enthusiasm signals an underlying passion. It is this passion we want to transfer to those who become our donor-investors.

Be yourself.

Among the factors that influence a person's willingness to give is the perception they have of the sincerity of the person calling upon them. People don't respond as well to people who are too slick.

While being prepared is essential, and being ready for the unexpected is important, part of the successful dynamic of a solicitation call is that you are yourself.

A story I often tell in my workshops is about a young Stanford volunteer who was assigned to call on an older person with seniority in her company.

She was reluctant to make the call, although she had done a good job building a relationship with the prospect. But finally we reached the point where the call had to be made.

While she hadn't made a gift of the size she was asking, she had made a significant "stretch" gift relative to her own capacity – she was what is called a "proportionate" asker. And she was going to ask her prospect to stretch as well.

At the moment of the ask, the woman froze slightly and blurted out the amount she hoped for. The prospect looked at her in stunned silence. Then he said, "I've never been asked for a gift that large before!"

And she, without thinking, responded, "Well, I've never ASKED for a gift that large before!" They had a good laugh. The tension was broken. She was herself, and he made the gift.

Remember that the solicitation call is really a conversation. It's an easier conversation if there are three people instead of just two. But, regardless, be natural, be yourself. It is an essential and powerful dynamic.

Be clear.

In everything you say or show to the prospect, be clear about what you want. At the outset, use open-ended questions to engage the person in conversation that reveals their thinking. But, beyond that, respect the time you have requested (30 minutes at the maximum) and make sure you clearly state what it is you want the prospect to do.

Among the specifics you'll want to include in your conversation:

• The amount of the gift you want the potential donor to consider;

• The area within the organization to which the gift may be designated;

• How the gift can be made;

• The impact the gift will have;

• The ways in which the person will be recognized if recognition is desired;

• The timing of the gift relative to the annual, capital or endowment campaign, and

• Any role you want the person to play within the organization or the campaign.

You don't have much time for this conversation but, if appropriately sequenced with your relationship-building activities, you really won't need much. And, if the prospect wants you to stay longer, be prepared to stay.

Be alert.

The best laid plans .... We've all had the experience where something goes wrong.

Good preparation can help remedy problems of our own making – for instance, the failure to present the right giving opportunity, not hearing what the prospect is saying, and the like. But it is just as important to recognize faulty dynamics that happen for reasons beyond our control.

People are reluctant to reschedule appointments, and often agree to keep an arranged meeting even when the timing is terrible. Watch for actions that indicate a lack of focus by the prospect: continuing to take phone calls, allowing interruptions from co-workers, unsubtle glances at her watch or the clock, shuffling of unrelated papers on the desk.

If this pattern persists, suggest that perhaps this isn't a good time for the meeting, and that you're happy to reschedule.

Often, the person is relieved, will confess to a problem that arose after the meeting was scheduled, and, in the next meeting, will be open, responsive, and grateful.

Be a good closer.

Don't leave anything open, unless the prospect hasn't yet made a decision. If she needs more time, find out how much. If he needs more information, get it to him as quickly as possible. If the gift is agreed to in the solicitation call, be sure you have a signed pledge form (if appropriate), or the gift, or have an understood process for how the gift will be made. Never leave behind an unsigned pledge card (you'll lose the reason for returning).

Be enthusiastic and appreciative of the gift (it's all right to be a little noisy now and then), but don't "sell after the close", that is, make a speech about the impact the gift will have in which you basically restate everything you've already said.

Make your exit smooth and gracious, and be sure the person receives a thank-you from you within 24 hours.

Lastly, remember that a new relationship has just begun and, rather than the job being over, it is just getting started in a new and better dimension.

•••

Understanding the dynamics of the solicitation call can introduce an element into the fund raising process that often eludes us: fun. Being part of the transformation of a prospect into a donor-investor requires a thoughtful transaction. These suggestions can help you be successful.

15

Conducting a Capital Campaign Feasibility Study

The debate about feasibility studies for capital or endowment campaigns goes on.

Some organizations shun them and still conduct successful campaigns; others that forego a study struggle and fail for lack of appropriate information.

To be sure, a feasibility study can be costly ($25,000 and up). But from a good study your organization will learn how it's perceived in the marketplace, which aspects of your cause or project to emphasize in your case statement, and potential objections which can be addressed in materials and meetings.

Further, individuals interested in leadership roles will emerge, you'll hear confidential feedback about the history or operations of your organization and, most importantly, you'll be able to gauge the inclination of individual and institutional funders to give to the campaign.

The following suggestions are offered for those still debating the options as well as those organizations that have decided to conduct a study.

You can't do it yourself.

Tempting as it is to save money and time, it's not an objective study if someone in-house conducts it. People won't be as candid with someone who's on staff, and staff people have a hard time staying objective in their questions and responses. Then there's the compounding matter that a good feasibility study assesses both *internal* and external readiness for a campaign. How can a staff member expect to be objective about himself and his superiors or subordinates?

Be sure you have good chemistry with the consultant you do choose, and that you're confident of his intelligence and ability to market your organization.

The need for good chemistry is true with any consultant you choose, but particularly for a feasibility study. Things have a way of getting delayed with a study (canceled appointments, changes in meeting places, appointments taking longer than expected to set up) and there's an ongoing need to work closely through some logistical minefields.

In choosing a consultant, it's also critical to choose someone in whose intelligence and ability to market your organization you have confidence. This individual (or his associates – be certain to meet them, too) will be the first contact with your potential funders. Be sure the person can master the information he needs to know, and that his style and personality will convey the integrity of the project or organization.

Require quantitative as well as qualitative questions on the structured questionnaire.

Statements in feasibility study reports like, "Most of the participants in the study supported the idea" or "Many felt this was not a good idea" won't satisfy the needs of left-brain (and many right-brain) board members who need to make a tough decision about a campaign.

Be sure the consultant includes scaled, weighted, and ranking questions to balance and verify the narrative questions. Then you'll have report findings that read, "Average assessment of the visibility of the organization was 2.2 on a scale of 4" or "The various campaign priorities were tested by asking the participants to rank them. In order of their ranking, the priorities selected were ...."

Ask to see a previous report prepared by the consultant.

Reports can range from 10 pages to 60 pages, be organized or random, specific or vague, include next steps or stop with the study's findings. Be sure to review a report before signing a contract. Also, be specific about what kind of report you want. Some organizations don't want a sheaf of papers; others won't feel they've gotten their money's worth unless they have a bound, thick study.

Be specific about what you want from the consultant.

Communicated expectations are the foundation of a successful consultant-client relationship. Be specific in your Request for Proposals (RFP), and repeat those expectations in your interviews and in the final contract.

Let the consultant know the maximum timeframe, what internal and external issues should be covered, the format you'd like for the report, and your understanding of the fee and payment structure. Have a signed agreement with a mutual termination agreement if the study must be stopped for any reason.

Work closely with the consultant at the outset of the study, to ensure that the right people are interviewed and that the consultant has the support he needs.

While the consultant should review the various segments of the constituencies to be included (business, social, educational leaders) and also provide the draft letter of invitation, the actual names must be generated by the organization. Of course, if the consultant is from the community, he can be helpful in providing contact information.

Have a point person on staff to respond to the consultant once the study begins. If the organization is setting up the appointments, communicate the schedule to the consultant in a timely way. If the consultant is setting the appointments, be sure the lists are accurate and that you've provided a signed copy of each letter on letterhead. In that way, if the consultant has to fax a second copy of the letter, he'll have one that's signed and appropriate.

Choose the signer of the letter of invitation carefully.

Many studies have fallen far short of their required interviewees because the wrong person signed the letter. Choose someone with visibility, connection with the organization, and who is well-respected.

In one study for a community cultural center, the mayor of the community signed the letter. There was nearly 90 percent participation. In another study, a controversial executive director became impatient and signed the letter rather than wait for the signature of the community leader who had been identified. The result: just 35 percent of those contacted agreed to participate.

Don't ask for results before the study is done.

It's not over until the last interview. Interim reports shouldn't be required (though you'll want progress updates. If something comes up during the study which is important for the client to know (for example, a foundation has said it will provide start-up funds if the request is made within 10 days), then the consultant will convey that information. Otherwise, sit tight and wait for the full report.

Require a verbal as well as a written presentation.

It's not enough to submit a written report. Your board should hear the results, and the consultant will want to present them. This is a major investment of time and money, and maximum board attendance should be encouraged. Provide an overhead or PowerPoint projector and ask the consultant to put the key points into graph form (this is where quantitative questions can really tell a story).

Whatever the outcome – do it, delay it, forget it – extract from the process those things which will benefit the organization in the long run.

Even in studies which say delay it or forget the campaign, the recommendations should provide a checklist and game plan for bringing the organization to the point where a capital or endowment campaign *is* feasible.

In one "delay it" study for an organization, the recommendations were sequential and comprehensive, allowing the executive director to use the recommendations as a plan for the next two years – checking off each recommendation as it was accomplished. At the end, the campaign commenced ... and succeeded.

•••

The benefits of conducting an objective feasibility study are many, and the majority of organizations conduct them before undertaking a capital campaign. However, each organization is different and some campaigns succeed well without a study.

16

The New Realities Of Capital Campaigns

Today's proliferation of capital campaigns is staggering, as communities respond generously and repeatedly to appeals for new buildings, expanded programs, and increased endowment.

While many of the conventional campaign practices are still important, times have changed, wealth has changed, and donors have changed. Most of it is good news, but new strategies and techniques are required.

Here's what you need to know about the new realities of conducting a capital campaign.

Look beyond the "usual suspects" to new donor profiles and patterns.

The transfer of wealth in our society, and the generation of new wealth from technology, biotechnology, and venture capital, have added a new and largely unknown layer of potential donors to most communities. And in spite of some economic wariness left over from 2000's bubble burst, elements of the boom have returned now. In fact, as of this writing, philanthropy is quite robust.

We're finding that many newer donors are responsive to broad issues rather than to specific organizations and locales, especially in terms of the environment, literacy, and certain health concerns. As a result, organizations are looking more and more *outside* their communities for people who share an interest in or passion in their particular issue.

Lead gifts represent a larger percentage of the total campaign.

Capital campaign literature used to advise that the lead gift to a campaign should be at least 10 percent of the total. That percentage has now increased to a minimum of 15 percent and, more likely, 20 percent. The impact? Organizations must have a lead donor securely on board before getting far along with their campaign planning.

A $25 million campaign to build a new facility for Alzheimer's research and care will require, in some instances, a lead gift of $5 million. A $200,000 campaign to repair the roof of a community church may require a lead gift of $35,000 or $40,000.

While not true in all campaigns, post-campaign analyses indicate that 90 to 95 percent of funding is coming from 5 to 10 percent of the donors. In one community campaign of $15 million, there were over 2,000 donors but *five* of them gave a total of $7 million (nearly 50 percent of the total).

There are still those organizations that can broker several smaller lead gifts into a pace-setting challenge to others, but the emerging pattern is this: one or more large gifts from individuals usually "seed" the campaign.

Donor expectations have changed regarding the "return" on their investment.

While recognition used to be sufficient (name on a building or classroom, creation of a scholarship fund), now donors are looking for solid evidence of "return." They want to know the impact of their gift, how well it is or has been managed, and how their investment has moved the organization to the next level.

Organizations that undertake capital campaigns must be prepared to provide a continuous stream of information and opportunities for their investors.

Hard-hat tours of new buildings, opportunities to meet and interact with scholarship winners, invitations to observe programs or classes are all part of the ongoing stewardship now required of capital campaign (and all) donors.

Those who give generously to your campaign may expect to sit on your board.

This is not, as many fear, "buying a board seat." This is acknowledging and respecting the desire of a significant donor to monitor, enjoy, and advise on her investment.

We need to remember that people give *through* us, not just *to* us. They're making an investment in their communities, and we're the vehicle they've chosen.

Competition has never been keener.

In communities across America and overseas, organizations that have never before considered a capital campaign are starting to feel that now is the time to get underway.

The combination of increased access to wealth, greater maturity of the nonprofit sector, and increasingly well-defined needs of communities, has led to the recognition of this time as a golden era for philanthropy.

But with it comes increasing competition for philanthropic

attention and investment. And understanding the environment for fundraising is as important as knowing the capacity of the organization to raise money.

The increased competition provides one reason to conduct a feasibility study. Although some experienced donors are reluctant to participate, feeling such a study is a waste of time ("Why don't you just come and ask me for the money – I know what you want"), it may be the only reliable way to uncover what's being planned by other organizations and which of your potential donors are already planning to support campaigns.

Public relations needs have changed.

Today, it's no longer enough to market or promote an organization. While some donors still respond because of their loyalty to a particular institution, the majority of newer donors are more responsive to issues.

Although it is true that the reputation and sentiment surrounding an organization may attract gifts from current or previous donors, you'll need to focus on the issues you're addressing to attract those who aren't aware of your impact in the community.

A campaign for a group that works with the aging should focus on the issues inherent in the mission, not just on the name and reputation of the organization: keeping frail elderly at home, dignity in the aging process, independence and quality of life, the increasingly aged population of America, and how their needs will have an impact on entire communities.

Donors are more issue-focused than ever before. Be sure your marketing addresses that.

Create a campaign leadership team that includes, but isn't limited to, members of your board.

Face it, your board wasn't recruited to run a capital campaign. Expect them to support it financially, and to be the decision-makers for major aspects of the campaign. But identify and recruit a steering committee, representing your constituency, to take on the fundraising and other aspects of the campaign.

In one campaign, the steering committee included a chair for major gifts, several members representing the regions served, the chair of the building committee, several lead donors, the chair of the board and the CEO, and those who represented other interest areas of the organization.

In another campaign, they were the "movers and shakers" willing to go out and ask for volunteers and money. In both cases, they took their direction from the board. And, in the latter case, on completion of the campaign several became members of the board.

Let your board continue to govern, and through the several board members who will sit on your campaign cabinet, keep the entire board informed about the campaign.

Acknowledge that you may need to be creative and flexible in soliciting gifts, especially from donors new to philanthropy.

This has several aspects. First, because donors seek organizations whose issues are important to them (in fact, many new family foundations prefer to approach nonprofits rather than the other way around) they're more ready to give at the beginning of the relationship than traditional donors. In some instances, the gift has already been decided when the contact is made.

This paradigm shift has changed research and cultivation dramatically. And, it has underscored the importance of consistent marketing of issues in the community. Only by persistent outreach can organizations attract the attention of those who can make investments but don't care to be actively solicited. These people don't need a long cultivation period. Put your energy into the follow up, not the lead in. That's the first big change.

The second shift may come in the terms of the gift. Savvy donors may be reluctant to hand over their well-managed investments to organizations whose investment policies or practices are unproven.

With these investors, you may need to work out an irrevocable pledge agreement that allows them to retain and invest the gift until you actually need it. This gives the donor confidence that he can keep investing the assets, but assures the organization the money will be there when needed.

Prospect to donor ratios are changing.

Capital campaigns are no longer the secret, quiet efforts they once were. Today, the "quiet phase" merely means "non-public." Quiet means we're going to the "friends and family" of the organization to solict lead gifts and test our goal before taking it public.

Because donor research has been revolutionized through the various wealth screening programs now available, we're able to identify the top donors earlier and more accurately. In earlier campaigns, where less was known about donors and our ongoing major gift fundraising was less active, we used to look at a 5:1 ratio of prospects to lead donors. Now, most organizations know who their lead donors are before they develop their campaign strategy. It's not unusual to have a 1:1 ratio – we know who our lead donors are, and they're already committed.

Today, the toughest challenge is the need for donors in the middle of the pyramid.

Pyramids these days look more like hourglasses. There may be a fair number of mega or transformational gifts at the top, and a flood of smaller gifts as the campaign rolls to completion.

129

Where the changes have been felt is in the middle band.

To remedy this, we need to be more deliberate in our stewardship of mid-range donors, and to be moving annual fund donors into increasing levels of recognition and engagement well before, and during, the campaign.

•••

Capital campaigns are the occasional efforts whereby we take our organizations to the next level of institutional excellence.

The new realities of campaigns make us mindful that donors are looking for a better, more engaging experience; that the old ratios don't work anymore; that campaign structure and cost are under increasing scrutiny; and that leadership, as always, is critical.

17

Recruiting and Retaining A Capital Campaign Committee

A major factor in organizing and running a successful capital campaign is the quality of the campaign's volunteer leadership. While the board retains final responsibility for overseeing the drive, the recruitment and retention of dedicated chairs and a strong and capable committee are essential.

There are two different kinds of general volunteer committees for capital campaigns: honorary and active. One is more window dressing, the other is the working committee. A two-tiered structure is quite common.

The honorary committee includes those individuals in the community who represent power, wealth, and long-term connection with the organization. They're the people who lead others to think well of your work and its importance.

But the real work of the campaign belongs to the active or working campaign chairs (usually two or more) and their committee. This committee, upon whose shoulders the primary responsibilities fall, may be called a campaign steering committee, cabinet, or council. Regardless of the name, these are the critical people without whom your effort will likely fail.

Here is what's important to know about recruiting – and retaining – active campaign chairs and a motivated steering committee.

The chair should inspire confidence, run a good meeting, and want to be deeply involved.

Your first step, when searching for the chair, is to identify a number of candidates for whom your campaign can become their top community priority for the next two to five years. This may in fact be the key determinant. If the leader lacks time, the job will fall back entirely on staff (making the campaign a difficult experience).

Among the candidates you identify (typically drawn from board members, former board members, advocates in the community, and major donors), you'll need to ask yourself some hard questions:

• Are they committed to your mission and enthusiastic about your organization?

• If not already on the board, can they sit on the board for the duration of the campaign (ex officio or as regular members)?

• Are they individuals who inspire confidence?

• Do they bring out leadership skills in others?

• Can they run a good meeting?

• Are they resilient, flexible, able to work with staff and other volunteers?

• Do they have a network they're willing to draw on to develop the prospect and volunteer base for the campaign?

• Do they want to be deeply involved with the campaign and your organization for the next several years?

Only those who match most of the criteria, should you

interview.

Recruit members of the steering committee both for their connection to important constituencies and for their skills in the various functional areas of the campaign.

Segment your important constituencies and identify the skills and experience you'll need (major gifts, planned gifts, endowment management) to tap into each specific group. Then, identify potential committee members who would be able to chair a committee of additional volunteers focused on that constituency.

In a campaign for a building project for an Episcopal cathedral, the chairs recruited representatives from the diocese, deaneries, and parishes, as well as those skilled in architecture, construction, major gifts, media, special events, planned gifts, and public relations.

Create job descriptions for both the chair(s) and the committee.

A job description serves as both a recruitment and management tool. Setting standards at the outset will spare you headaches later.

Start with the committee job description, and be unequivocally clear about responsibilities, reporting (to whom, how often), expected outcomes, time required, and duration of the assignment.

When that's done, develop the chair's job description including specifics described above. Both descriptions should begin with a thank you for volunteering, a short (!) summary of the campaign purpose and intended impact, and a few words about the importance of their involvement. The descriptions should be reviewed and approved by the board, and then used in enlistment of the committee and chair.

Set a meeting calendar for the year and stick to it.

Busy people like to set dates on their calendars well in advance. Choose the second Tuesday or third Friday at 8 a.m. or noon or whatever works for your committee. Meet monthly throughout the campaign, taking August and December off if possible. Subcommittee meetings should also be scheduled 12 months out. And do everything in your power to stick to the calendar.

Secure the financial commitment of the chair(s) and the campaign committee before you ask them to ask others.

In a campaign, it's essential to solicit the board first, and then to involve the board chair in soliciting the campaign steering committee chairs. The chairs then enlist and solicit their committee; and those committee members in turn solicit their committee members.

Every solicitation of a campaign leader (including all committee members) should be done in person, even if the stretch gift involved isn't a "major" gift to your campaign.

Give assignments to all members (no free rides).

On a capital campaign committee, all members should have subcommittee and solicitation assignments. Subcommittee assignments may include major giving, community outreach, marketing, special events, and other activities related to the campaign.

When organized in this way, the campaign committee remains more strategic, leaving the detail work to the subcommittees. It becomes, in effect, a steering committee overseeing all the activities of the campaign.

These subcommittees will have volunteers who are not on the steering committee, people from the community who increase the campaign's reach.

All members of the campaign committee need to carry their weight through chairing or serving on one of the subcommittees *and* in making solicitations as appropriate and requested.

Keep meetings focused on both the mechanics and the impact of the campaign.

Just as all board meetings should have a "product demonstration" (otherwise known as a "mission moment") to keep the passion stoked, so should campaign steering committee meetings.

Be sure each meeting features a short presentation by a client, program staff person, community member, or someone who directly or indirectly benefits from your work. This will remind everyone of your organization's impact in the community and will keep the engines humming.

Otherwise, the mechanics of the campaign (list review, problems with construction, delays in pledge fulfillment) can diminish the energy of committee members and potentially dampen their enthusiasm for asking.

If enthusiasm lags, determine the reason and fix the problem – or de-enlist.

If a committee member begins to slip in his responsibilities, address the situation immediately. Have the chair of the steering committee call and learn why.

If the problem can be fixed (poor communications from staff, unhappy about a lack of support from her volunteers), devise strategies to fix it. If it cannot be fixed (new job, new baby, no longer interested in the organization), then the steering committee chair should de-enlist the committee member and thank him for his service.

Quite often when a meeting is held with a committee member who has disengaged, that person will beat you to the punch and resign before you even have to ask. However, if you do have to ask, a gracious way is to thank the person for the time he's given, say you sense he has other priorities keeping him busy, and ask if you might replace him on the committee. If he protests, then set some concrete expectations .

Be sure the committee's relationship to the board is clear and observed (the board is not off the hook just because there is a campaign committee).

The board has ultimate responsibility for the success of the campaign. The campaign chairs are recruited by the board chair, and one of the chairs should sit on the board either as a member or ex officio for the duration of the campaign.

Board members should serve on campaign subcommittees, and are expected to make solicitations. The fact that there's a steering committee doesn't reduce the board's responsibility. It simply shifts the authority for ongoing campaign business to a board-appointed committee that duly reports to the board at every meeting.

Celebrate them at every opportunity.

If you want to keep the chairs and committee motivated, celebrate them often. Stay informed about the progress of their calls, and reinforce their success and efforts (even if unsuccessful).

Think of ways to provide incentives for completing the calls (something similar, perhaps, to the "You've Earned Your Spurs" certificate for volunteers described in an earlier chapter).

One steering committee chair brought a box of Kudo candy bars to each meeting, and would give "kudos" to those who had made a difficult call, completed a difficult negotiation, or in other ways pursued their leadership responsibilities.

We tend to think of the big celebration at the end of a campaign: that will come sooner, and with a much more loyal and renewed group of volunteers, if they are celebrated all along the way.

•••

Campaign success is measured in several ways: dollars raised, donors increased, visibility enhanced, and the expansion of volunteer leadership. Creating and retaining strong leadership will help you accomplish all of these goals.

18

Transformational Gifts

Transformational gifts became front-page news during the latter part of the 20th Century. They were varied in purpose and dramatic in impact. They came from individuals or family foundations and from people new to philanthropy.

When the economy tightened after the technology collapse in the late 1990s and then September 11, these gifts slowed. But now that the economy has recovered in large part, the incidence of these gifts is once again rising.

The obviously transformational gifts are huge. Warren Buffett's announcement in June 2006 that he'd be giving $31 billion to the Bill and Melinda Gates Foundation is an obvious example. His gift will transform the Gates Foundation and the programs it operates and funds.

Joan Kroc's bequest to the Salvation Army ($1 billion) and National Public Radio ($200 million) were clearly transformational. Others, such as those given in previous years by the Gordon and Betty Moore Foundation ($650 million to Cal Tech) and the late Bill Hewlett ($400 million to Stanford University) were also headline-worthy gifts.

But transforming gifts are also gauged by their relationship to the overall scope and budget of the organization. We can read about these in every issue of the *Chronicle of Philanthropy*. In a recent issue, 22 gifts were listed of $1 million to $25 million for organizations ranging from universities to an independent school to an art museum). Drawn from several years of research and thinking, here's what you should know about transformational giving and how to position your organization to attract such gifts.

These gifts come from philanthropists of all ages and experience.

An analysis of gifts over the last decade would show transformational gifts coming from:
• The cyber- and venture-capital rich
• Women
• Ethnic and racial groups previously under-represented in philanthropy
• Those who have become wealthy through the inter-generational transfer of money underway in America. And,
• Those who have made large fortunes (think Warren Buffett) and want to give back to the society that helped them succeed.
The old methods for identifying, cultivating, and even soliciting don't always work. Many of the newer philanthropists are inexperienced donors, and don't show up on the usual lists. Further, they often seek out organizations and don't want to be sought out themselves.

This isn't your father's philanthropy – it's more like your mother's.

An interesting phenomenon of transformational giving is that it patterns women's philanthropy. We know that women tend to get involved first, then make a financial commitment. Traditional male donors, on the other hand, have often made a gift first

139

(particularly when asked by a peer) and perhaps become involved on the board later.

New philanthropists – particularly those making transformational gifts – want to be involved with both defining the gift and the institution it will transform. In other words, the desire for involvement both precedes and follows the gift.

A gift of $150 million to Stanford in the 1990s from Jim Clark was the result of three years of conversation, exploration, communication (much of it by email), and program definition. Clark's involvement as a former professor was coupled with his gratitude for the opportunities Stanford had provided him to develop the research leading to the founding of his successful companies.

There are countless examples in recent decades of sustained involvement by major transformational investors in the organizations they've funded.

Transformational donors invest in issues and ideas – not just in institutions.

Interviewed in an annual report of the Community Foundation (Silicon Valley) several years ago, one young couple, Ray and Joanne Lin, put it this way, "We fund change, not charity."

Another philanthropist, a young woman who established her own foundation, commented in response to a question regarding the kinds of organizations she funds, "I don't fund organizations, I fund issues."

While traditional "community philanthropy" – the funding of the basic arts, health, education, social services – is still important to experienced philanthropists and many new donors, there is this trend towards looking for the organizations that address issues (children, homelessness, poverty, domestic violence, substance abuse) and funding them not because they're familiar to the donor, but because the issue is important.

This shift puts a new emphasis on the marketing thrust for nonprofits: the focus has to be on the mission (the need that's being met, not the need you have for money) and the values implicit in that mission.

Too often, mission statements and marketing pieces focus on the organization, and not on its values and results. In 1989, the late Peter Drucker, always wise and prophetic, commented in *The Wall Street Journal*, "People no longer give to charity, they buy into results." He was ahead of his time.

Transformational giving, because it transforms organizations, will often attract funding for both infrastructure and programming.

Capacity-building grants are becoming more common. Community and other foundations have been providing "technical" or "management assistance" for years but now individual and family foundation funders are also investing in stability.

They're doing so because the issue being addressed is so important, and funders are willing to invest in ensuring the organization has the internal systems to support continued fulfillment of its mission.

In one such instance, an organization with strong mental health programs highly dependent on government funding was given both a program grant and an organizational assistance grant by a family foundation.

The rationale was made clear in the grant: the mission of the organization was important to the funder; the dependency on government funding was a concern to them; the creation of a separate foundation to raise and manage private funding was essential to the future health of the organization; and current staffing needed assistance to create that foundation and get the fundraising started.

**Transformational donors have some exciting character-
istics – ones that are changing the face of philanthropy as
well as the institutions and communities in which they have
invested.**

These are the principal characteristics that emerged in the
research, observations, and interviews conducted for the book,
High Impact Philanthropy, which I co-authored with Alan
Wendroff in 2001.

• Transformational donors invest in results and in the values
implicit in those results.
• They seek values-driven organizations, often without
realizing the values are what's attracting them.
• They want organizations to accept their ideas and opinions,
not just their money.
• They're impatient for results – and sometimes for the ask.
• They're willing to make longer term investments.
• They want to transform institutions and society.
• They often want a base of power in the program or
organization.

These attributes in some cases represent a confirmation of
more traditional philanthropy, but there are several with broad
implications for the way nonprofits must retool some of their
approaches. The next several points deal with these implications.

**If your organization wants to attract a transformational
gift, it must focus on results, not needs.**

A 1999 article by Scott Kirsner in *Wired* highlighted the
philanthropic leadership of Steve Kirsch, founder of Infoseek.

The description holds true for many of the newer philanthropists. Kirsch, according to the article, "likes groups that are ambitious, he wants his money to make a measurable difference, and he prefers that the altruism be balanced by sound business sense. He likes being intellectually stimulated by what he underwrites."

The article went on to say: "... the new breed of high tech philanthropists want to reinvent the art of generosity. They share (Kirsch's) sense that simply giving money away is too passive and uninvolved. They want to lend business expertise, identify and support 'social entrepreneurs' hungry to shake up the nonprofit world, and quantify their results. In short, they want to create a new kind of charity. But they don't call it that. They call it venture philanthropy."

Our sector has two bottom lines: financial and values. We must show results in both. For the financial we provide numbers; the values are shown in both statistics (how many are helped, how many lives are enhanced) *and* stories (about the real people behind the statistics).

If your organization wants to attract a transformational gift, it must focus on the issues, ideas, and values inherent in the mission.

Often this starts with reevaluating the mission statement. Is it so corporate that it only conveys what your organization does, and not why you do it? If so, chances are it doesn't convey your values.

We function in a message-driven society – so much so that it takes up to seven exposures to a message before it can break through the resistance we've developed.

But, advertisers who seek consumers for the purposes of having them spend thousands of dollars on cars, high tech gadgets, and other such indulgences, aren't shy about talking about values long before they mention their product.

Consider this advertising insert which appeared in several magazines with affluent readership during the boom years of the late 90s:

> "We build walls. With our everyday routines. And our cram-it-all-in schedules. Walls that make a nasty habit of separating us from our dreams. But, what if there were no walls? What if there were a way to break straight through to your dreams? There is. All you need is an outfitter with the right equipment. Ford is your outfitter. Outfitting you with the most far-reaching sport utility vehicles on earth. Climb in. And watch the walls come tumbling down."

So little mention of the cars; so much emphasis on the values.

But in our sector we don't need a huge advertising budget to get a message across. Integrate your values even into the smallest unit of your outreach. Stanford University Libraries sent this simple thank you card to its donors: A sketch of the library was on the front of the fold-over card. Inside, the text read: "Your gift to the Stanford University Libraries helps us assemble the sources, the arguments, the hypotheses, the wisdom and controversies of the ages. For all those here and those yet to come, please accept our gratitude."

It was signed by the University librarian. Even the simplest expression can convey your values.

Transformational gifts may be decades in the making, or they may come in more quickly than you can imagine.

Many times, transformational gifts aren't known until we're notified. They represent decades of involvement or observation by the donor, and a decision to make a lasting investment in an organization.

These kinds of gifts are more the product of faith in an organization's ability to continue operating and acting long after a person has died.

Contrast that with other transformational gifts. Sometimes, like Buffett's gift they come as a surprise to all except those closest to the donor. Because they are issues-focused, or about change, they have an urgency about them. The urgency is based not on the organization's perceived need for money, but on the donor's perception of the urgent need the organization is meeting.

Other characteristics of transformational donors provide additional reasons for looking carefully at your cultivation, solicitation, and stewardship systems.

Even traditional donors who decide to make a transformational gift are increasingly impatient with the pace of the nonprofit sector and the bureaucracy of some institutions. And, younger donors are very impatient, particularly those who have worked in high-tech fast-paced start-ups.

When they want information, they want it by return email or phone call. The process inherent in so much of what nonprofits have traditionally done in donor development may have to be accelerated.

Internalize the steps in the development process (identify, qualify, develop strategy, cultivate) and skip past those that seem unnecessary. And, if suggestions are made about speeding up processes or stripping out layers of bureaucracy, listen to these advisors. They've known success either because of their creation of wealth, their emergence into mainstream philanthropy, their climb up the corporate ladder, or their management of inherited wealth.

They are looking to make long-term investments – some are using the venture capital model of a minimum three-year investment – but they want short-term results and a non-bureaucratic environment in which to be engaged and savor the impact of their giving.

If you remember five "I" words, you'll be better positioned to engage a potential transformational donor.

Convey Impact, focus on Issues, offer opportunities for Involvement, remember that this gift is truly an Investment, and practice Innovation.

•••

These suggestions will, I hope, give you a platform for action. In communities around America (and increasingly, other parts of the world) there are individuals and foundations with wealth that wish to invest in their communities. Position your organization to be an agent for their dreams.

19

Implementing a Successful Year-End Fundraising Program

There are two "year ends" for most nonprofits: fiscal and calendar. We raise money during both. The former helps us to close the year well. The latter allows donors to give during the most active time of sharing in our country – November and December. Whether your fiscal year is just underway, half-over, or coincides with the end of the calendar-year, it always seems to spring upon us fast. And almost anytime is a good time to begin planning year-end appeals.

While it's tempting to do the same things over and over, particularly if they're seemingly successful, it may be time to freshen up your practices.

Here, then, are the most important things to know about putting your year-end campaign on more innovative footing.

Take time to analyze last year's successes and failures.

Be willing to take a hard look at last year's campaign before starting this year's. Figure out what worked, and be open to admitting what didn't.

If you had one volunteer who, quite frankly, made most of the personal asks, that's an area needing attention. If your donor acquisition mailing lost money for the third year running, analyze why. Look at the lists you're using. Talk with your mail house. If your renewals are down, review your message. Maybe your letters have a dunning tone, rather than one inviting investment. Or perhaps they focus on your institutional needs, rather than on your results.

For those with a large donor base, consider a donor focus group. You'll identify more clearly what motivates your constituency and be able to incorporate what you learn in your future appeals.

Take time to develop a year-end plan with goals, objectives, and action steps.

When your analysis is completed, develop a solid year-end plan. Too often, for short-term funding efforts, organizations set aside the formal planning process and "just do it."

But a plan provides internal guideposts that keep any initiative on track, and also gives volunteers a sense of the importance of the year-end campaign and of their involvement.

Cover all the strategies you'll use: mail, phone, personal solicitation. Cover all constituencies: individuals, corporations, and small family or private foundations.

It doesn't have to be an elaborate plan, but it should have dollar, donor, and other goals; measurable objectives; and an easily understood action plan boiling down each task to who will do it, what resources are needed, and the date by which it needs to be done.

This becomes the "battle plan" for the duration of the campaign, and is a document reflecting both the professionalism of your organization and the importance you place on clear communications. At the end of the year-end campaign, it's also the basis on which you'll conduct future planning.

Crown the plan with one energizing strategy.

For one organization, it was the introduction of thankathons as follow up to the year-end campaign. For another, it was the first-time development of personal solicitation teams. For yet another, it was bringing in an outside trainer to provide personal solicitation coaching for volunteers and staff.

Other innovations might be a mini-retreat for campaign volunteers to review the plan; recruitment of a "creative team" to review themes and messages before the campaign is launched; having a "PS-athon" allowing board members and other volunteers to add personal notes to letters.

Recruit a team of volunteers that represents a good mixture of ideas, energy, and vision.

Veterans of your year-end campaigns – whether current or former board members, development committee members, or community leaders who work with you on an ad hoc basis – will learn from and be inspired by new faces and ideas around the planning table.

These new people bring perspective and experience from other organizations they've served, and have the ability to ask the obvious questions that veteran volunteers may be too reluctant to ask ("Why do we do the campaign in July rather than September?" "Have you ever tried having teams of volunteers who compete with each other for results?").

At a recent public television meeting, staff people were excited about the ideas an array of board members from across the country brought to some of the nagging issues they've been working with for years. Their ideas had worked at museums and colleges and schools, and now it was apparent they were going to be tried in the public television arena as well.

Assign volunteers to areas where they will flourish.

Whether they're new to your campaign or veterans, chat with all of those you're enlisting and find out what motivates them. Just because someone has typically had a particular role in your campaign doesn't mean that's the role she wants to continue.

Many are uncomfortable making face-to-face solicitations, but are confident initiating phone solicitations. Others despise the phone, and prefer to write or sign letters. Still others know that face-to-face is the only kind of solicitation that really builds relationships.

By determining individuals' talents and comfort zone before assigning tasks to them, you can avoid having to hover, cajole, or de-enlist.

Provide volunteers with training and coaching.

If your volunteers are training-resistant, call it something else: leadership session, campaign planning, strategy session.

Of course you can't enforce a "mandatory" session, but it should be one of the items stipulated in the recruitment process. And, even if your volunteers have been engaged in fundraising for years, convey to them how this session will focus on new ideas and approaches; will review the goals and deadlines; and is an opportunity for them to be mentors to new volunteers.

One-on-one coaching is also a critical aspect of raising the volunteer comfort level. With coaching, the volunteer meets with the staff or volunteer leader and reviews the specific aspects of his or her solicitation assignments. Like training, this is done as close as possible to the time the solicitation will be made.

Conducted properly, training and coaching will be seen increasingly by volunteers as a "perk" – and some of the skills you'll convey (listening, questioning, closing) may also be skills your volunteers can apply in their paying jobs.

Be enthusiastic, even if this is the umpteenth time you've done a year-end campaign and it feels like "same old-same old."

There's nothing more dampening to volunteers and other staff people than cynicism about a campaign, prospects, or the process. Whatever needs to be done to keep the enthusiasm up, do it. Set up a hotline with another development officer or executive director and share your gripes with them.

Educate your entire organization about the year-end campaign's activities, and how they can be part of the development team.

One way to maintain your own enthusiasm is to create a development-team feeling within the organization. Program staff people can be great resources for mailings, personal visits, and corporate or foundation proposals. But if they feel imposed upon or uninvolved, they won't be effective.

Their perception of development may be based on a belief that it's only about asking for money. But in so many other ways they can be a key part of the team: providing information, being at the organization for tours or teas, or speaking informally or formally in the community.

One organization put out a "Good Newsletter" every week during its campaign – a single or double-sided desktop report placed in everyone's mailbox. It listed the gifts, the totals, told funny or warm stories about staff and volunteer experiences, and generally conveyed the complexity of the campaign while focusing on results. The support that development received from program and administration staff increased substantially.

Be sure your donor recognition and stewardship program has been reviewed for its successes and weak points, and that levels and practices are appropriate for your donors.

In your analysis for year-end campaign planning, don't neglect recognition and stewardship.

Look at your recognition levels and verify that they still fit the pattern of giving in your organization. See if people are getting "stuck" at particular levels and consider ways of encouraging them to increase their gifts.

Ask your donors about their experience with you. Do an informal stewardship survey. Have cards on the table at events asking people what other kinds of activities they would enjoy. Find out if your communication is too much, too little, and done with the right medium.

Overall, we need to remember that the real "return" on investment isn't the mug, the tote bag, or the free tickets. It's the knowledge that a gift has made an impact in the community. Don't overly focus on tangible benefits. Instead, devise recognition and stewardship that's mission-anchored and reflective of your organization's values.

Stick to your deadlines, and plan small celebrations when each milestone is reached.

When the year is over, the year-end campaign is over. While most organizations keep their books open for a few days into the new year to record gifts that came in during the holidays, the active campaigning is finished.

Take time to celebrate. It's a festive time of year for most people, and these celebrations needn't be elaborate. Gauge your celebrations against measurable objectives: dollars raised, contacts made, parts of the campaign completed, or an extraordinary gift or experience.

These can be spontaneous or planned, large or small. They don't even have to be done in groups. A celebration can also be sending flowers to the first volunteer to complete her assignments.

Some organizations regard celebration as an intrinsic part of their culture; others have to be persuaded that taking time to savor success is important. Whatever it takes to build celebrations into your campaign, it's worth doing so, as they energize and motivate and the benefits will far outweigh the time they involved.

•••

A year-end campaign is vital to the financial success of most nonprofits. By building in these strategies, the campaign can also have great benefits in team-building, perception of professionalism, and increased donor, volunteer and staff involvement.

20

Soothing Disgruntled Donors

It happens to all of us, no matter how hard we try. We upset a donor. Wrong name on the envelope. Writing "Mr. and Mrs." long after a death or divorce. Acknowledging the wrong amount. Misspelling a donor's name in the annual report.

While any of these mistakes may be harmful, they don't necessarily sully your relationship for the long term.

Here's what you should know about picking up the pieces – and soothing a wronged donor.

Admit the mistake.

Searching for someone else to blame may make you feel better, but it doesn't soothe the donor. Donors see our organizations as functioning teams.

Telling a donor you'll find out who made the mistake isn't the point. Apologize, tell the donor you'll find out why the mistake happened, and make sure it doesn't happen again.

Don't Argue

Never argue with a donor. Accept their version of the mistake

– even if you sense it isn't entirely accurate. Acknowledge the donor's anger with phrases like, "I can imagine how you feel..." or "I don't blame you for being upset..." or "I can understand why you're thinking these things about us...." All of these phrases are safety valves for the donor's anger and open the door to conducting a constructive conversation.

Let your staff know this is a serious matter.

All too often, the seriousness of a mistake doesn't sink in. Sometimes, it's hard for people to understand why a donor doesn't just laugh it off or grin and bear it.

Part of creating a culture of philanthropy in your organization is focusing on donors and their needs. The vast majority of donors not only need to be treated with respect (and continued mistakes connote disrespect), they don't understand when organizations repeat the oversight or error.

Use incidents to instruct staff. Use them to initiate a data base cleanup or other solution to the problem.

Let the donor know what you're doing to correct the problem.

Admitting the mistake is good; letting the donor know that his experience has led you to examine the cause and correct it, is better. That alone can help a donor feel as though his experience has had a positive outcome.

Don't let data entry slide, even if you're short-staffed.

I know, I know: I've seen the change-of-address forms and other information piled high next to the data entry desk (while every support person was deployed pulling lists, running reports, and doing other urgent work).

Nevertheless, correcting your data base is vital, and reminds us again and again of the difference between what is seemingly urgent and what is truly important.

When a donor has informed you of a change, or an envelope has been returned marked "Deceased" – enter that information on a regular basis.

Only by keeping the data base current can you, with confidence, apologize to a donor whose information has been mishandled or not updated.

For serious lapses, have an immediate "response team" ready.

Publishing names that were to have been anonymous, failing to direct a donor's gift towards the program designated, omitting a person's name from a recognition list – all of these require more than a phone call from someone working at the membership or development support desk.

For these lapses, an internal meeting among staff leaders should be followed by an offer to visit with the donor and explain how the error occurred.

If a visit isn't welcomed or possible, be sure it's the CEO or Vice President for Development, or even the Board Chair who extends the apology by phone or handwritten personal note.

Consciously connect accuracy and timeliness with the whole issue of stewardship in your organization.

In too many organizations – particularly large ones – we tend to separate personal stewardship from the nuts and bolts of data base maintenance. This can be particularly true at universities and medical centers where data bases are often maintained by people who aren't daily connected with development.

But, in truth, accuracy and timely generation of receipts is connected to the whole area of stewardship. If our goal is to convert donors to investors by building relationships with them, remember that the relationship begins by getting the name right and letting the donors know as quickly as possible the gift has been received.

We have, unfortunately, drifted far from the old 48 to 72 hour rule for acknowledgments, citing the difficulty of processing gifts through often elaborate systems. Still, we need to figure out how to put the donor's needs ahead of the system's complexity.

Recognize and reward those whose accuracy and timeliness – and donor satisfaction quotient (DSQ) – is consistently on target.

We spend so much time troubleshooting problems that we often neglect those who do their job well. Set incentives for achieving a "zero margin of error" environment by celebrating those people whose accuracy and timeliness are impeccable.

The resources we dedicate to solving problems could be minimized if we focused on putting those same resources into systems and encouragement that will ensure a low rate of mistakes.

Be honest with yourself about the ability of your software to handle the size and complexity of your program.

We put off upgrading our systems because conversions are painful and costly. But faulty systems lead to situations with donors that can be significantly more painful and costly!

Far too many organizations persist in using outdated technology. Set about finding the resources to get a new data base management system or upgrade your existing one. This isn't a luxury, it's a necessity.

Check those mailings before they go out – many disturbing errors can be caught.

Signing letters in a hurry without looking at the salutation, rushing a mailing without checking for duplications, and failing to match thank-you receipts against the original list of gifts reflects a practice that many now-defunct technology companies embraced: there was never time to do it right, but it seemed as though there was always time to do it over.

Do it right the first time, so that you won't have to correct your mistakes – and the bad feelings they engender – over and over again.

•••

To donors, there's no such thing as a "little mistake." They expect more of us. You may lose the donor no matter what you do. But by honest and diligent follow up to the problem, you can do a great deal to keep that individual connected to your cause.

21

Starting a Stewardship Program

Stewardship, the continued involvement, cultivation, and care of those who give to your organization, is the most important practice in the development process.

It's an organization's philosophical commitment to the value and importance of donors as well as their gifts; a belief, an attitude, that each donor – whether individual, corporate, or foundation – contributes more than money, and that gifts are a symbol of his or her belief in the values, purpose, and importance of the organization.

Donors who feel they're valued only for their gifts, or who feel neglected after giving, quickly sour on an organization or even the nonprofit sector as a whole. Whereas donors who are drawn deeply into a relationship through effective stewardship become advocates and promoters.

Imagine the best scenario possible. With your various year-end giving efforts you acquire 100 new donors, renew several hundred more, and upgrade still hundreds of others. What happens after the thank you letter is sent?

• How are you going to involve those individuals in a way

that will let them know you regard their gift as a symbol of their faith and appreciation in your ability to meet a particular need in the community?

• How are you going to let them know during the year that you regard them as partners in providing essential services?

• How are you going to let them know that their gift is being used appropriately, and that you regard it as an investment in the community, not just in your organization?

Here's what you should know to get on the right track.

If your board hasn't adopted a policy regarding stewardship, start by creating and approving one.

Many boards don't really understand what stewardship is all about. Therefore, a policy that implants the importance of donors and stewardship securely into the systems of the organization is a sound first step.

By ensuring that a board policy is in place, stewardship is more apt to be a steady practice, rather than an occasional spurt of activity.

Once you've done this – which will require some education about stewardship from staff at another organization perhaps – then you're ready to get started.

The policy will become part of the culture of your organization if there's a plan to go with it.

Organize a stewardship planning task force involving board members, other volunteers, a development or administrative staff member, and several donors.

Involving donors in such a process is particularly important, as they have the particular perspective you're looking for. Give them a leadership role, and let them be a part of the team that presents the proposed stewardship program plan to the board.

That plan should include the following:

- An analysis of the current donor base according to the way gifts cluster.
- The creation of four or five giving (recognition) levels based on where the gifts cluster.
- Naming of the recognition levels. Avoid being too clever or too complex. If possible try to keep the names linked to the mission; otherwise use generic names such as donor, patron, benefactor.
- Determination of the "benefits" for each level. These should be kept mission-related and should reflect IRS guidelines regarding the value of "givebacks."
- Review and approval by the development committee of these levels and benefits.
- A mechanism for monitoring the relationship between stewardship and recognition.
- An annual evaluation process that reviews the program, benefits, and impact of stewardship.

Begin involving donors with their first gift.

If you wait until a donor reaches some magical, internally designated threshold of giving before you start practicing thoughtful stewardship, it may be too late. This is why "thankathons" were invented. When groups of volunteers, staff, or program beneficiaries get on the telephone to thank donors, good things happen.

Donors hear personally that their gift is appreciated and will be used wisely. Callers have a chance to talk to other donors in the community, and the shared enthusiasm is mutually beneficial. A deepening involvement can occur on both sides of the telephone connection.

Always done in addition to a written letter or receipt, the thankathon is a key element of effective stewardship.

Stewardship becomes evident to donors when you alternate your messages to them.

A trusted rule says that for every one time you ask someone for money you should contact him or her two other times without asking.

There are various ways to achieve this. Ask for your donor's opinion by sending out a proposal or brochure with "DRAFT" stamped on it.

Put together a focus group around a new program initiative or funding possibility and include your donors.

Send out occasional "white papers" treating an issue your organization is dealing with locally and relate it to a larger national or international issue by including a thoughtful article or newspaper clipping. Draw the donor's attention to what you're doing locally to address this critical issue, and let them know their gift helps make that possible.

If you don't allocate money in your budget for stewardship, it won't work.

Make stewardship activities – donor receptions, special mementos for large gift donors, dinner or refreshments for a thankathon – an integral part of your development program budget.

The budget for special fundraising activities or events is always easier to justify than the budget for donor development. Fundraising results are usually immediate and measurable. The impact of donor development groundwork may not be evident for years.

But donor development – and stewardship as a primary function – is what drives successful fundraising. While difficult to measure precisely in its financial return, stewardship affects the entire bottom line. And an overall increase in giving and a growth in donor retention will follow if it is done consistently and well.

Implement stewardship practices appropriate to the amount of the gift, your budget, and your image.

Donors are uneasy when they believe a memento or event is too expensive or inconsistent with their image of the organization. They wonder if their gift has been used up by its acknowledgment.

Scale back the tangible benefits accorded to donors and focus on communicating the real benefits: the impact of the gift on the fulfillment of the mission in the community.

Don't assume everyone wants to belong to a "giving club." Many don't. Instead, they may want to enter into some other kind of interaction with the organization.

At the time the gift is made, find out how the donor wants to be recognized and involved. Make that information part of the database, and update it regularly through your ongoing relationship with the donor.

Be aware that some larger donors wish to be left alone except when *they* initiate contact. They will set the schedule: you simply need to be ready.

Combine cultivation and stewardship activities as much as possible, as the two functions are highly related. And, put donors and non-donors together at special events.

A favorite cartoon shows a woman putting place cards around a large, beautifully appointed table. She is saying, "Donor, non-donor, donor, non-donor...." She is, of course, exactly right. Mix those who have given with those who are still considering a gift. The results will be beneficial to the individuals and to the organization.

If you're going to maintain relationships that will benefit the organization over time, continue your stewardship practices even when an individual's giving flags.

As a rule, we base our stewardship strategies on internal measures such as the size or frequency of the gift. In most cases, this is appropriate. But board and staff should remember that a donor's circumstances may change temporarily.

It is foolish to abandon the relationship with someone who has given significantly in the past but has cut back or stopped giving. Remember that gifts are investments. They have a residual impact. The return is evident long after the gift has been made.

If you have a good relationship with donors, you should know why they've changed their giving patterns. Chances are they'll be back – but not if you cut off your contact with them.

When creating stewardship programs, remember that people give to and become involved with your organization because of the program.

Create opportunities for donors to get to know the people who are using their investments to create and deliver your programs. Involvement is deepened, and commitment enhanced, when donors become partners with those who actually provide the service. Only then can they understand how their values are being acted on.

•••

Competition for resources in the nonprofit sector will increase as traditional sources of funding shrink. Donor loyalty is a known factor in successful organizations. Maintaining that loyalty is the principal goal of stewardship, and is its most powerful result.

22

Using the Internet for Stewardship

Volumes have now been written about using the Internet for fundraising. Most nonprofit websites offer ways to donate via the Internet, and the incredible outpouring of philanthropic gifts after the Tsunami in South Asia and the hurricanes Katrina and Rita were for the most part made in this way. Even some very large gifts (six figures) were given via the Internet following these natural disasters.

But little has been written about the effectiveness of the Internet in helping to retain donors once a gift has been made, and how to integrate the Internet into your overall stewardship plan. This chapter offers a brief look at the key points about using the Internet for sustaining (and growing) relationships with your investors.

Learn the right technology for "email blasts" before jumping into Internet stewardship activities.

Few things are more irritating than getting an email that you know has been sent to 500 other people – all of whose addresses are there for you to see. There are numerous software programs and simple techniques for avoiding this mistake – find out about them and choose the one that works best for your budget.

An email is personal mail – and you want a stewardship message to make the recipient feel special. While the donor may know intuitively that others are getting the message, it's still important that he or she not see the list you've sent to.

Segment your donors by interest for maximum effect.

If like most organizations you have multiple programs to stimulate donor interest and investment, create your email stewardship program around those interests. Tailoring your email message is as important as tailoring a renewal letter: people like to know that you know whom you're sending a message to.

If yours is an orchestra with an education program, identify the donors who will be most thrilled by an announcement that one of the schools you serve has received a special citation for its music program which was, according to the principal, stimulated by the efforts of your orchestra.

Capture the interest areas in your data base, and then tailor the emails to the donors' interests.

Keep it short and sweet.

Use a spiffy subject line so people will open your email, and keep the message to a minimum. You'll be amazed: a 10-line email with a powerful story will be read – and sometimes forwarded – whereas a longer message will often be bypassed and deleted.

What does a message contain?

Remember this is stewardship. It's not a request for money,

nor a sterile update on some aspect of your program. This is about excitement and conveying return on investment.

Tell a story and engage the reader in the role her gift has played in making something happen. Relate how an autistic child had a communications breakthrough because of the additional staffing you were able to provide as a result of the donor's generosity.

Tell the story of the impact of your science programming on a kindergartener – and how that turned into a wonderful teaching moment at a school you serve.

Let your subscribers and donors know what happened at a Saturday matinee when children who'd never seen live theater were transformed because tickets were made available through their generosity.

Always include a thank you. And, never include an ask. This is not Internet fundraising – it is Internet stewardship (the gifts will come later, and be larger, because of the stewardship).

How often is too often – and how much is just enough?

As with any communications, if you have something to say, say it. If you don't, withhold the urge. You should aim for at least quarterly communication by Internet with your donors – but if there's *legitimate* good news in the interim, send it.

Cyber stewardship isn't random – it should be part of a strategic "moves management" or other donor development program.

Be strategic in your plan for all stewardship, including Internet stewardship. Tailoring the messages by interest area is the first step, but there's also the matter of:

Timing - If your donor traditionally gives in December, then make sure he receives a stewardship email sometime in February and then quarterly thereafter.

Integration with other stewardship techniques - Use other forms of stewardship, of course: donor appreciation events, e-newsletters or regular newsletters. Make a plan that includes Internet communications as part of the overall stewardship.

Interactive communication - When communicating regularly by stewardship email, ask every so often for a response (which will give you greater knowledge about the prospect). This can be about receiving further information, continuing to receive emails, or probing for questions they may have about your work.

Be careful about assuming that your older donors don't use email, and take every opportunity to build your list.

Years ago, when the whole Internet buzz began, we somehow got the idea that only younger people would respond to email messages. How wrong we were! The number of grandparents who keep in touch with their grandchildren or their far-flung family and friends by email is growing exponentially.

Be sure that every communication (newsletter, website, thankathon, phone appeal, special event registration, annual fund giving form) offers a place for recipients to send their email address to you "for purposes of communicating with you economically, efficiently, and with occasional snippets of good news."

Expand your donors' knowledge and sense of engagement by providing links within the message.

Better than burdening people with a long email, use links to articles or information that the curious donor can pursue. Be sure the stewardship message is sufficient to convey gratitude for the gift and a story describing its impact, but include a link if appropriate (perhaps to a recent newspaper article about you, or another website connected with your work).

Internet stewardship isn't just for people who give via the Internet – it can work for all your donors.

Major donors who are solicited personally, people who give via mail or phone appeals, as well as people who give through your website will all feel more connected when they receive your email stewardship notes.

Some organizations even use this method for keeping in touch with their planned gift donors, letting them know when a bequest has matured and made a significant difference in the organization and thanking them for including the organization in their estate plans.

•••

As the Internet prevails – and is joined by cell phone communication, iPod messages and other rapidly evolving methods of communication – its obvious use in raising funds should be joined by the equally obvious benefit these new media have for letting people know that their gift matters and, more importantly, that *they* matter to the future of our organization.

23

Evaluating Your Fundraising Effectiveness

Sometimes, in the urgency of moving on to the next fundraising activity, analyzing the success of the previous one is overlooked. Did we raise the money? If so, what worked that we can do again? If not, what was the problem?

There are many ways to evaluate your fundraising effectiveness. Within the profession, benchmarks have been set. There are general formulas for calculating the cost of fundraising, and there are organization-specific standards regarding the number and size of gifts you should bring in annually, and what constitutes a reasonable donor retention rate.

Taking these "hard" factors into consideration is of course important. But there are other elements, too, some of which are "soft" and less measurable. Factor these into any evaluation of your development program.

Without a balanced view of what constitutes effectiveness, it's hard for development committees or boards to know if their fundraising efforts are working. And, it's difficult for development professionals to engage volunteers around an appropriate set of goals.

Here's what you should know about both the "hard" and "soft" sides of evaluating your fundraising effectiveness.

Set annual fund raising goals that are an "attainable-stretch."

Too often, fundraising goals are set by boards or administrators without the benefit of previous (and anticipated) performance indicators. They establish a goal that fills the gap between earned revenue and what's needed to run the organization, without regard to whether it's possible to raise the funds.

Setting a fundraising goal demands the involvement of development staff and volunteers in a careful analysis of previous campaigns, a survey of the current environment, and a review of prospective, current, and lapsed donors.

It also requires knowledge of how many volunteers will be available for face-to-face visits, and what financial resources are needed to conduct direct mail campaigns, telefunding, or stage large-scale fundraising events.

Stretch goals should be set systematically, not arbitrarily, and then actively pursued.

Acknowledge that fundraising events are best categorized as "friend raisers," and set your measures against two goals: to raise as much money and as many friends as possible.

Many organizations rely heavily on fundraising events. This often leads to disappointment, because event fundraising is subject to a host of perils, including timing, unexpected costs, lack of publicity, uneven volunteer leadership, and other hard to control factors.

However, if fundraising events are seen for their other

primary value – as friend raisers –then plans for measuring their effectiveness take on a new dimension.

Viewing events as friend raisers as well as fundraisers requires greater planning: attention during the event to those who are being cultivated as well as those who already have a relationship with you; post-event debriefs among volunteers and staff regarding what they saw and heard; and follow up with attendees through thank-you letters, phone calls, and future involvement.

An important measure of fundraising effectiveness is how thoroughly the board and development committee own the goal and are involved in its achievement.

Fundraising cannot be considered effective when development professionals single-handedly – or with very few volunteers – raise all the money.

Truly effective programs are those that involve board and other volunteers as well as administrative and program staff in the planning, implementation, and evaluation phase of any drive, whether annual or capital.

Board members are the nucleus of any fundraising program. They must own it. And when they do, they inspire other volunteers to get involved, and buoy staff enthusiasm.

Fundraising effectiveness should also be measured by how many board members and other volunteers are willing to make face-to-face asks.

Board members and other community volunteers are the best people to contact others in the community. It isn't enough to write notes on letters or even to make phone calls. A mature fundraising program measures its effectiveness not only by money raised and calls made, but by how many people were willing to sit down with prospects and donors and ask for a gift.

Personal solicitations drive down the costs of fundraising by engaging volunteers in asking current donors for large gifts and balancing the high cost (at least $1.25 for each $1 raised) of donor acquisition through direct mail or paid telephone solicitations.

A good fundraising program should raise your visibility in the community as well as increase donors.

Raising money is just the beginning. An annual program puts the mission out into the community and helps raise the visibility of that mission and the organization.

In one campaign involving two organizations that worked with women and children who had experienced domestic violence, a local advertising agency donated spot video and radio announcements as well as newspaper advertisements.

Their theme was, "Breaking the Cycle of Violence." It was a blockbuster campaign and helped the two organizations significantly increase community awareness. They also raised a considerable amount of money, which the two organizations shared equally.

The retention rate of donors is a critical measure.

If you have to start from scratch every year, trying to convince people to give, then your fundraising program isn't very effective. The reason, usually, is because the focus is on raising money, not on building relationships.

It's important to remember that donors are really investors: when they make a gift, the relationship begins (or renews). They're interested in the impact of their gift, the results the organization achieves, and they want to hear from you about the difference their gift has made.

If you don't communicate with your donors until the next solicitation, it conveys the idea that you're only interested in their money – not in letting them know you acknowledge their gift as a symbol of their belief in your purpose and your results.

Be sure your fundraising program is balanced, relying on funding from a variety of sources.

Most organizations have had to get away from government sources as primary funders, but find themselves overly relying on another single source like foundations or corporations.

It's dangerous to rely on one primary source of funding at the exclusion of others. If that source bottoms out, the overall effectiveness is jeopardized. Be sure you're cultivating and soliciting from *all* constituencies.

In an effective program, people feel good about giving, and asking.

This is the softest, yet the hardest measure of success. If your volunteers and donors feel good, and you raise the money you set out to raise, then the program is effective at building the organization, community awareness, and the likelihood of continued investment in the organization is great.

If your volunteers are irreparably burned out at the end of an annual or capital campaign, it hasn't been effective no matter how much money you've raised.

Renewal of volunteers is essential. Along the way, they're bound to get tired, frustrated or discouraged. However, staff and board leadership support for volunteers should be such that these feelings are fleeting.

Recognize your volunteers in the way that's appropriate for

their accomplishment and personal needs, mete out their assignments so they aren't overwhelmed, help them when they seem discouraged, provide professional advice and counsel to help them improve their skills, give them training and coaching to improve their effectiveness, and let them know how important they are by measuring the impact of their service in terms of the accomplishments of your organization.

Remember that there are two bottom lines in philanthropy: the financial return and the values return.

In an effective program, both bottom lines are honored and strong. In reporting your results and measuring your effectiveness, measure not only the money, but the impact on the mission as well. The mission embodies the needs of the community and inspires the investment.

An effective fundraising program is based on a belief in the importance of the mission, the urgency of the need that's being met, and views all gifts as investments and all donors as values-driven investors.

Honor the gifts and the values they represent, and, when reporting your successes to your donors, remember to tell the stories that convey the impact of their generosity. It will be the highest measure of your effectiveness.

•••

There are many measures of effectiveness in fundraising. Take them all into consideration when setting your goals, monitoring your programs, and conducting your campaign evaluation or year-end reporting.

24

Hiring Development Staff

Making the right hiring decision has always been tough. But to make matters worse, we've seen a recent shift from a buyer's market to a seller's market in nonprofit development positions.

Even a casual reader of any publication listing development-related job openings is aware of the shortage of qualified people.

Increasingly, professionals in search of staff find themselves looking to sources outside the sector, often with a great deal of worry about how people without development experience will fare in the nonprofit pressure cooker.

Others network intensively with fellow professionals, but are fearful of the risk in raiding another organization's staff.

Still others put off hiring, waiting for the market to break, and use consultants or volunteers to keep the annual or capital funding programs afloat.

The reasons for the shortage, and for our inability to bridge the gap between openings and people to fill them, are complex. Some have to do with the way our sector is viewed, some with the way our organizations are perceived to be managed, some with lower than market salaries, and some originate from the way we manage the hiring process.

Here's what you should know about hiring development staff, especially if it's a tough market in your community.

Be sure the job description is current and clear.

This seems so elementary you're wondering why it's included here. The truth is, most job descriptions are poorly thought out. If the job is a previously held one, the tendency is to "find Ruth's replacement." No attempt is made to figure out if Ruth was doing the right job for the organization.

Resist this tendency and instead give yourself the luxury of some zero-based thinking: what tasks do we need to do, who are our existing people, what are their talents, how would they like to be assigned, what would motivate them and, given that we need an additional staff person, what should that job be?

This can be an energizing process for staff members.

By the same token, if the job is a new position, develop the job description in consultation with existing staff. What do they see as the best role for this new person?

While you're drafting the job description and ad for this position, do some internal marketing with the board and administration to raise the respect and the salaries for the development function.

We spend most of our time marketing to our community, and too little time letting people within our organizations know the impact of the development function. I'm not suggesting you become a shameless self-promoter, ultimately doing more harm than good.

Instead, you'll do yourself and fellow staff a favor by continuously communicating within your organization the grants you bring in, the major gifts you've cultivated, the increase in membership, the visits from dignitaries and funders, and favorable press that might have been missed.

Position this new or just-vacant job in the context of everything you're accomplishing, and let people know how important it is.

Also, take a look at all salary and benefit packages in the development office, compare them to similar organizations in your community, and attempt to persuade the budget-makers that this position, in order to attract the caliber of person needed, should have a higher salary.

Look for potential candidates outside the traditional sources and experience pools.

Development is a challenging job: we all know that. And because we tend to focus on knowledge and experience rather than the *qualities* of a person, we get frustrated when we don't find that ideal fit.

In my years of hiring I've found that even if a person lacks experience, I would rather have someone who's smart, flexible, and motivated rather than a technician who knows how to conduct a direct mail campaign but lacks the qualities to make her a success in the organization.

Think about the backgrounds and experience that can transfer to our sector: marketing, advertising, teaching, other professions that require communication and the ability to work with a wide variety of people and situations.

Look beyond our sector for experience. You just might find an ideal candidate with little or no development experience but in whom you see great potential and are willing to train.

Look for qualities, not just qualifications.

People fail in jobs not because they attended the wrong university or don't have the requisite three to five years

179

experience at a similar institution. They fail because they don't have the intellectual or interpersonal attributes, or a sufficient energy level, to get the job done.

Harvard professor Harry Levinson provided the employment world with the behavioral job description decades ago. In this approach to defining a position, Levinson admonished managers to define not only the knowledge and experience required, but also the intellectual and interpersonal skills and the energy they're looking for. It is around these qualities, Levinson asserts, that most failures occur.

Take time to define the qualities as well as the qualifications, and circulate these among the people who will be interviewing your candidates.

Get some training in interviewing.

Most managers are miserable interviewers. We give away the store by telling candidates too much about the organization at the outset of the interview – and then are thrilled by how well they match what we're looking for.

We telegraph answers ("Here at Children's Services International, we look for people with high integrity and great flexibility in their work style. Are those attributes you would bring to our organization?"). What do you think they're going to say to that?

We talk too much, and don't listen.

Often, we attain our interviewing skills as managers by remembering those who interviewed us. But most of them had no training, and were making it up as they went along.

But you can do better. At the very least, thumb though a professional book for some suggestions and guidance.

Make sure the hiring process has integrity and shows respect for the candidates.

Too many organizations display arrogance in the hiring process, albeit inadvertently. By failing to communicate with candidates about the process, keeping them waiting, putting them through poorly structured interviews, not letting them know whether they're still a candidate, and by not thanking them graciously for their time, we convey arrogance and an impression of our organization (and our sector) that is irreversible.

Remember that hiring is a marketing process for you and for the nonprofit sector. The person you don't hire today may be tomorrow's gift prospect. Be sure she leaves with a positive feeling.

Involve the right people in the interview process, but don't go overboard.

It's important that final candidates interview with the people who'll interact with them. The board chair, development chair, CEO, CFO, and selected others need to participate.

However, don't make the process so complex that it appears you're syndicating the risk of the hiring decision.

Some companies and nonprofits have literally dozens of people, individually and in panels, who meet with final candidates. But ultimately this dilutes the decision-making process and can convey to the candidate that yours is an organization that has difficulty making decisions and taking responsibility for them.

Keep the process swift but thorough, and keep it on a timetable that you convey to the candidate.

Be honest and open with final candidates.

If you have a great candidate you want to hire, by all means sell her on the sector and the organization. Tell her about the passion and the satisfactions, let her know there are nonmonetary compensations for working in the sector that ultimately are more valuable than money.

But, while doing this, don't paint a picture that slights the truth. In our attempt to sell a promising candidate, we tend to gloss over the very things that'll eventually be points of concern or departure: the real expectations.

This has to do with everything from describing the issues around the workload, to working with the board, to accurately depicting the organization's fiscal stability to the idiosyncrasies of your board or staff.

Transparency is in. Let your new employee become a partner in implementing your mission by presenting portions of the job as a pleasure filled with opportunity, but revealing the parts of the job that will be a challenge. No surprises, please.

Once the person is hired, give him a decent orientation and start-up period.

When I transitioned from a development director's job in social services to a development position in higher education, it was a big shift. And, yet, when I arrived at the new job on the first day I had flowers, but no boss. He was away for a week. No one really knew I was coming (he had sent the flowers by wire), and the first week was utterly frustrating.

I found my way around, but missed that welcoming immersion that sets the tone for the way people interact.

When a person is welcomed, introduced, oriented to the facility and to the administrative and program staff – and assured that there's a support system within the organization – then higher productivity and confidence result.

Be diligent about the separation of board and staff responsibilities.

One sure way to cause a talented person who's new to our sector to quit prematurely is for the board to micro-manage individuals or departments.

Hiring a new person is a good time to have a quick session with the board about the line of demarcation between board and staff. By tying the discussion to the new position, it seems less of a lecture and more of an orientation for the board.

At the same time, be sure that board members don't perceive increased staff as decreased responsibilities for them. In fact, it may mean increased responsibilities. If you, at last, are able to bring on a director of stewardship, then board members will be much more actively involved in the stewardship process.

•••

Transitions in staffing, while time consuming and sometimes difficult, can be opportunities for redefining *all* jobs, not just the one being filled. Even though other job descriptions may not change substantially, people will feel as though their job has been reaffirmed.

This exercise may even lead to the happy conclusion that you can promote from within, thereby giving others incentives to stick around.

25

Hiring a Development or Organizational Consultant

At some time or another, nearly every nonprofit needs a development or organizational consultant. It may be for a capital campaign, for strategic planning, to facilitate a board retreat, or to conduct an assessment of development systems and practices.

Making the decision to bring in a consultant is relatively easy. A situation or opportunity arises within the organization that, by its nature or requirements, requires outside assessment, counsel, or facilitation.

But while the decision to hire may be easy, the search can be quite confusing – especially if it's the first time you've sought counsel. Just sorting through the array of consultants is itself a challenge.

As you would expect, consultants come in all sizes, shapes, and dispositions. Some call themselves organizational consultants, some say they're development consultants, others are planning consultants, and still others are fundraising or campaign consultants.

They may be from a "one-person shop" or part of a larger firm with local, state, or national offices. They charge by the job, the day, the month, or the hour. Some incorporate expenses, others itemize them, still others build them in as a percentage of the contract.

The duration of a consultant's service will also vary widely. Some consultations are as short as a half-day (board or staff training session) and others go on for years (board development, staff development, capital campaigns). Some have ironclad contracts that reflect legal training or advice; others operate on a verbal contract or handshake.

With all this variation, it's important to know some basics before hiring. Here, then, are important things to know about hiring a development or organizational consultant.

Before approaching any consultant, be sure your outcomes are clearly identified.

Then you will know – from the confusing array of consultant labels – whether you need development, organizational, strategic planning, or other kinds of consultation.

Identifying your desired outcome also helps you create better measures for the interview process and for the eventual evaluation of the consultation.

If, to use the example of a board retreat, your objective is to identify basic goals for a strategic plan, to create closer communication among board members, and to build board and staff understanding of mutual responsibilities, then you can ask the consultant directly how he or she would facilitate each of these outcomes. Obviously the interview will be more revealing, and the decision easier, if these specifics are discussed.

It's relatively easy to find information about consultants.

If you're part of a formal network (AFP, CASE, NAIS, AHP), there are usually local or national consultant directories available (and some are on the Internet).

In many locations, community and private foundations maintain a consultant directory with listings according to types of consulting and typical clients and fees.

In a growing number of communities, there are nonprofit management centers that also have lists of consultants. Some even provide consultants directly, often for a lesser fee than an independent consultant charges.

Informal networking is also effective, of course, and colleagues in other organizations will usually give you candid information about consultants with whom they've worked.

Mistakes in hiring a consultant hurt the organization in two ways: the time and money are wasted and, later on, when a consultant may be needed again, no one wants to hire one.

The process is simple. When you have completed the research to see who provides the kind of consultation you need, develop a list of individuals who seem, by experience or reputation, to fit what you're looking for. Have a mix of big firms and independent consultants, which will allow you to compare resources and approach.

Conduct telephone interviews (they provide an initial insight into the candidate's communication skills). If you like the telephone session, ask for a written proposal (these offer insights into organizational skills, respect for deadlines, verbal skills), and then follow up with a face-to-face interview.

If the consultation will involve the board, be sure the key players on the board are involved in the interview. If the consultation is for a capital campaign consultant, include key development, administrative, and board representatives in the interview. And, remember, focus the questions around your desired outcomes.

Sadly, consultants can be viewed as a threat. If their purpose isn't explained, and if there's no knowledge of or buy-in for the goals, it can lead to a lack of cooperation based in fear or resentment. Discuss the proposed consultation with staff. If it's for strategic planning, tell them what the process will be (interviews, meetings, a retreat) and the approximate duration of the process. Let them know how much time you'll expect from them.

If it's for a capital campaign, be clear at the outset how demanding a campaign is and why a consultant can help achieve the goals and relieve the chaos.

Some consultants, because of their experience or reputation – or because of the length of their contract with you – will require large budget allocations. Therefore, the importance of the outcomes to the overall capacity of the organization needs to be stressed.

Too often, communication about a consultation is only with the development office or administration. Program staff also need to be informed.

These decisions are highly specific to each organization. The person who was just right for one organization may be completely wrong for another. Know your organization, and what it needs.

Sometimes, it's hard to know what's best. An organization with a fragile infrastructure that's approaching a capital campaign will have to "assemble the bicycle while riding it."

If, however, the board is comprised of people impatient with process who just want to get out and ask, a phased consultation using two distinctly different individuals may be in order. One would work systemically within the organization; the other would go out into the community with board members and raise the money. One process (and consultant) is transformational; the other is transactional.

187

Know what you need before choosing your consultant.

Some consultants are compelling and charismatic in their presentations, and it's easy to get swept up in their vision. This quality is worthwhile, particularly for facilitation or training sessions with board or staff.

However, somewhere in the interview ask to review the details of the consultant's proposal: fees, contracts, schedules, staff resources in their offices, and timelines, including other consulting work that may delay yours.

Knowing this information prevents you from getting your heart set on a consultant who's too busy or one you can't afford.

If this is a long-term capital project, starting with a feasibility study, where the consultant will have a great deal of interaction with your board, staff, and the community, be sure the person wears well.

Talk to others who have used the consultant. Conduct more than one interview. Be certain the chemistry checks out with the key players on your team. Also, if you've chosen a larger firm, and another consultant is going to work with the lead consultant, it's important to meet that person as well.

Related to this issue is the importance of determining who spends what amount of time with you. There have been unfortunate situations where the lead consultant didn't show up at all after a time, leaving the project in the hands of a second consultant who didn't have the chemistry or experience to give the client confidence.

Draft a Letter of Agreement or contract, no matter how short the consultation is.

It is tempting, with a board or staff retreat or training, simply to make a verbal agreement or to trade e-mails. But it's important to have a letter of agreement or contract for every outside service you engage.

In this letter or contract you include the desired outcomes, the client and consultant expectations, timeline, conditions for termination of the agreement by either party, fees and expenses, amount of time to be spent by the lead consultant, and other pertinent information including a description of the "deliverables."

It needn't be complicated or prepared by a lawyer. But the completed letter of agreement is a way to keep the consultation on schedule. It signals the importance and professionalism of the consultation, and provides excellent recordkeeping for both parties.

If the consultation is long-term, build benchmarks into the agreement to measure progress.

Long-term arrangements of any kind tend to drift if they aren't evaluated periodically. If, going into the agreement, the client and consultant know they're going to be working together for a period of years, incorporate benchmarks and review periods into the contract.

Benchmarking can be done in one-on-one meetings, or can be built into quarterly or semi-annual sessions with the board.

Some contracts can be written so that the consultation is in phases, with evaluation criteria established for the completion of each phase.

Once you've hired the consultant, and if you expect the individual to keep up his or her side of the bargain, be sure you keep up yours.

There are numerous ways that client actions or delays can

derail or destroy a consulting arrangement.

If a consultant needs information to prepare for a meeting, delays in receiving it can throw a timeline into disarray. For example, clients that agree to release invitation letters for a feasibility study at a certain time – a time pegged to dates the consultant has kept open to conduct interviews –can delay the study by months if the letters aren't sent out on schedule.

Failure to inform the consultant of changes at the organization or of events that have bearing on the consultation can put the consultant in a difficult position with key individuals whose confidence is critical.

Maintain agreements, keep promises, and make sure the consultant has both the environment and the tools to be effective. Oh yes, and please pay your consultant on time.

•••

Engaging a consultant, at the right time for your organization, can be enormously productive and effective. These suggestions I hope will help you make a better decision and help you manage the process more ably.

26

If You Want
To be a Consultant

Nearly every development professional I know has at some point considered becoming a consultant. It's seen by many as a way not only to escape the pressures of the daily grind but also to choose one's own venue, supervisors, and colleagues. New people, an array of fascinating places – the view is extremely tantalizing.

As with all decisions, however, there's an upside and a downside to becoming a consultant. Over the years, I've given countless information interviews to those exploring the wider world of consulting. Here's what I advise them.

To be good at consulting, you have to like change.

As a consultant, you're a change agent. Your job is to do what no one on the inside of the organization has been able to do. Further, you have to like steady change – places, people, challenges.

In a typical week you could be in a museum, a public television station, a social service agency, or an independent school. You could be working with board members, CEOs, development officers, or non-board volunteers. Your challenges may include strategic planning, major gifts counsel, board retreats, or campaign feasibility studies. No day is like another, and no situation is the same.

You have to be flexible.

When people ask me what are the top traits of excellent development officers, I always include flexibility. It's also true for consultants.

Recently, a client who had casually mentioned the need for a campaign plan "down the line," called me on a Thursday to say (with desperation in her voice) that she had just been told she needed the plan by Monday.

I canceled my weekend calendar, arranged a conference call with the client and her supervisor for Friday, determined the scope and format of the plan, and set to work. I sent off the plan by email on Sunday night and on Monday morning heard from the client.

Were they pleased? "Thrilled" is how she described the reaction. If I hadn't been flexible, much would have been lost. For them, and for me.

Managing several clients at once takes getting used to.

Shifting gears in a regular job – from the annual fund to the capital campaign to a board retreat – is relatively smooth. You know the organization and the people.

As a consultant, you make those frequent shifts with a different set of circumstances and players. It's imperative to keep one organization separated in your mind from another. Each situation requires your full engagement and full knowledge of the operating context. Either you thrive on this, or you find it exhausting.

Shifting gears as a consultant is definitely a "0 to 60 in 30 seconds" challenge.

Travel is part of consulting, and it's no longer glamorous.

If you travel only occasionally, you can steel yourself for today's heightened security and the delays that accompany it. But, if you decide to consult outside your hometown, you'll be getting on and off airplanes with regularity. You can either be very Zen about this, or troubled by it.

I tolerate the challenges of travel because that's how I can do what I do. But if travel makes you weary, and you still want to be a consultant, you'll sharply narrow your base of clients by simply staying in your own locale.

There's a big difference between working on your own and working for a consulting company.

The biggest difference is marketing. A consulting company will market you; on your own, you market yourself. And that takes a special talent ... and considerable time. Another difference is that a consulting company may absorb some of your overhead including benefits. For many, working for a consulting company is a step towards working on their own. It's a smart way to test your comfort level with this line of work.

Consulting offers you an opportunity to focus on what you enjoy and what you do best.

In a day-to-day staff job, each of us has activities we put off till the end of the day, week, or year. As a consultant, you can define what it is you do best and like to do most. That's not to say you'll like every element about an assignment, but for the most part you can focus on what it is you love to do.

For me, never having to organize another special event was a great lure into the world of independent consulting. I attend them happily, but I simply don't plan them anymore.

Concerns about the financial risk of working with nonprofits are largely unfounded.

In my nearly 20 years of consulting, I've worked with hundreds of organizations and had only two clients that didn't pay. In one case, the person who had hired me left under hostile conditions and the organization refused to honor her commitments. In the other, the organization never had the money to pay me to begin with. I wrote both off and the experience didn't discourage me.

You won't make as much money as commercial consultants, but your sense of satisfaction will be great.

The same values that brought you to the sector in the first place should guide your decision to consult. There is huge satisfaction in seeing new ideas and creative solutions at work in an organization.

Although some nonprofit consultants generate good fees, and your daily rate may climb with your reputation, you'll probably never make what your colleagues in the for-profit arena earn.

Nevertheless, nonprofits are increasingly willing to pay more for quality work. Assuming you're capable, of course, you'll eventually find financially stability. As importantly, you'll be highly fulfilled with the impact you're making.

While establishing yourself, agree to a certain number of "business development" conferences and programs to get

194

your name out.

If any one thing set me on my path towards building a solid client base, it was my frequent appearance at conferences for which I was paid little or nothing (sometimes a small honorarium, usually travel expenses).

If you aren't comfortable as a stand-alone speaker, get yourself invited on professional panels at local or national conferences. When people hear you, they may resonate with your message and your style.

But be forewarned: it can take a long time before any of these attendees contact you. Although conferences are strong business builders, you won't often make an immediate sale.

Effective consulting is a combination of skills, chemistry, timeliness, delivery, and quality.

The right skills may get you hired, but mutual chemistry is essential for the assignment to work. And, no matter how good you are, you must respect deadlines. Why did I give up my weekend to write that campaign plan? Because I value the client and because I've worked with one of their development officers off and on for more than 10 years. Timeliness, delivery, and quality governed my creation of that plan and I was motivated knowing they were depending on me. Forty pages later, they were thrilled. And so was I.

•••

Am I a satisfied consultant? Yes. Do I ever wish for the days when I worked 40 or 50 hours a week instead of 60 or 70? Not really. Do I advise a consulting career for everyone? Clearly not. There are those for whom consulting is entirely the wrong choice. But for those who can withstand the challenges and thrive on change, nothing is better.

27

Strategic
Institutional Planning

To plan, or not to plan? Alas, that is no longer the question. The mandate is clear. Nonprofits are expected to have timely and relevant strategic plans. Accountability and results are in; fuzziness and generalities are out.

While passion and faith still motivate our volunteers and donors, they like these feelings to be anchored in facts. They want to be reminded of the mission and vision and what we're doing to achieve both.

Prospective board members want to see the plan; potential investors want to know what we'll do with their money. Internally, the management team needs a roadmap.

And the most useful tool for systematically accomplishing all of this is a solid strategic plan – one that involves both staff and board in the preparation, implementation, and evaluation process.

Here, then, is what you should know about the importance of strategic planning and how to engage board and staff members in the process.

Market the importance of planning to both board and staff.

There are those who believe that plans are worth little more than the paper they're written on. These are usually the freewheeling, self-described "creative" people who contend plans inhibit their freedom to innovate. In fact, most who use this excuse are really saying they don't want to be accountable. They don't understand that systems liberate.

Convincing these individuals to plan is a challenge. It may take time, or a crisis, or some straightforward internal marketing of two concrete benefits of a well-formulated strategic plan:

• It conveys the vision, mission, and program goals that inspire people to give and serve.

• With a solid financial plan attached, it's a key internal tool for maintaining stability and strategic direction, and an important external tool for attracting funders and volunteers.

Learn to identify the sources of resistance to the idea of a strategic planning process, and prepare responses to those objections.

Both board and staff may resist planning for one or more of the following reasons:

• Answering pressing needs and problems takes precedence over the strategic planning process;

• Staff leadership is concerned about board member involvement in program planning and worried about issues of staff accountability;

• Board members are impatient with the planning process, feeling it requires a time-consuming analysis and discussion of issues they feel are obvious;

• Previous plans have gathered dust on the shelf and participants in earlier processes feel their efforts were wasted;

- The organization seems to be functioning well without one ("If it's not broken, why fix it?");
- There's a latent feeling by the board or staff leadership that the organization is so fragile that planning would be fruitless (as one board member remarked, "rather like rearranging deck chairs on the Titanic");
- The organization's board and staff leadership just don't know how to begin the process.

If you don't find ways to address these points of resistance, the plan will never happen. A good starting point is to find an example from your history or that of another organization which confims that plans are not only needed for consistent management, but also for board and donor engagement.

With staff members, provide assurances that the board isn't taking over the management of the organization.

This can be a tough hurdle in some organizations. Worried that board members may get too "hands on," staff may resist having board members get involved in planning.

Assure them that, ironically, this is less apt to happen if the board is informed and involved in the planning process as well as the plan's implementation. Board members who watch from the sidelines tend to get more easily angered or frustrated than those who are players in the game.

Provide staff with a clear picture of the role the planning task force and the entire board will play: lay out the steps from initial meeting through implementation and annual evaluation of the plan, and show how the partnership will work.

With board members, give them a clear definition of their role in the process, and how they'll work in partnership with the staff.

198

Some board members will understand this right away; others may either be reluctant to get involved or anxious to take over the process. Neither role benefits the process.

The best way to gain buy-in from those responsible for implementing the plan is to form a board/staff planning task force responsible for conceptualizing how this will be done. Appointed by the CEO or board chair, with a specific job description, this task force initiates, guides, and oversees the completion of the plan. When recruiting, let each member know why they've been selected and what expertise or perspective they bring. Give them the planning schedule and deadlines, and provide samples of previous plans from your organization or other organizations.

Often, the people chosen to serve haven't worked together before. One independent school, formulating its first strategic plan effectively used its initial meeting as an opportunity not only to get acquainted but also to set the deadlines, and delienate the process.

These parents, faculty, administrators, and former parents achieved a strong sense of commitment from this first meeting, and then met frequently and productively to create a forceful plan. The advantages of such a diverse representation became apparent as the areas of previous conflict were ironed out in a collegial way.

Even if they understand their role, board members may still need to be convinced of why they need to spend their time in this process.

Each board is different, of course, but among the most persuasive arguments for getting people involved in the planning process are the following:
- The board is ultimately responsible for the mission and vision of the organization and the strategic planning process

encourages careful evaluation of both.
  • Boards are able to govern better when they understand the process and the assumptions behind the strategic plan.
  • Because board members are removed from day to day operations, they bring a broader view and can be unencumbered change agents.
  • As fundraisers, advocates, and ambassadors for the organization, board members must be involved in the planning process so they know what's going on with the organization.
  • Board members provide a "window" into the community. They represent important constituencies and, without them, the planning process depends too heavily on "mirrors" for program and service evaluation;
  • Board members' skills and experience add value to the planning process.

Have an agreed-upon approach and use everyone's time wisely.

Remember that all nonprofit activities essentially cluster in three areas:
  Program (including facilities)
  Organization (board and staff development), and
  Development (donor and fund development, marketing, public relations)
  Years ago I began using these three areas as the template for the "Tri-POD" approach to planning and it has worked for many organizations.
  As for using everyone's time wisely, make sure of the following: that all meetings are necessary; that your deadlines are well-conceived and serious; and that you use a facilitator to get through the tough parts of the planning (the priorities and the allocation of resources).

Choose a leader, or co-leader, who not only is committed to planning but is strong enough to keep the process rolling.

Planning thrives or fails based on the quality and determination of the leaders. It also helps to have thick skin and broad shoulders.

Planning ignites passions and uncovers biases and emotions. Rejected ideas inflict hurts and frustrations, and long-held (but now perhaps irrelevant) dreams become insistent. The talent for listening, incorporating points of view, allowing the forum to unfold, and for helping people feel valued (even when their ideas are rejected) is critical.

The leadership can come from the board or the staff – and co-chairs representing board and staff can work wonderfully. But be as certain as you can that the individuals meet the criteria stated above. And be sure your co-chairs share one vision. Otherwise, you may end up with conflict at the head of the table and dismay all around.

Communicate progress to those who aren't involved on the task force.

Planning may be an alarming process for board and staff who aren't seated at the table. Devise ways to communicate during the process and, within defined limits, invite feedback at interim steps in the process.

Involve constituencies in "market" research to be sure their needs and ideas are reflected in the plan.

No strategic plan is complete without a framework of what the community thinks, wants, and needs. An independent school surveyed faculty, parents, former parents, and schools that their graduates attended. A Boy Scout Council conducted phone and in-person interviews with current and former leaders, past and present Scouts, as well as community leaders. A consortium of public school educational foundations surveyed its members and non-member districts.

The feedback from all of these surveys was used to validate existing goals and create new ones; it also provided valuable ideas for new strategies that addressed a changing marketplace.

Use the plan once it's done.

This may be the single biggest way to convey the importance of the process and the product, and the value of board and staff involvement. Don't let the plan gather dust. Use it. Challenge it. Revise it. Evaluate it honestly.

If it isn't working, roll up your sleeves and address what is wrong. If it's lack of commitment, get your staff and board together and explore why. If it's overly ambitious and people are staggered by it, tone it down. Put some of your goals or objectives off until the following year. If it seems inappropriate due to internal or external changes, revise it.

Plans aren't carved in stone. They are vital living documents meant to be revised.

•••

In today's demanding nonprofit world, we have no choice but to create strategic plans. We must be entirely accountable, and willing to convey our impact and our results.

To be successful, planning must be viewed as important. To be accepted as important, planning must be successful. And, success will depend on your ability to bring board and staff together in the process, and to listen to your community.

28

Be Resolute

Most of us have had our patience, fortitude, and confidence tested in recent years. We've watched a volatile economy erode and then rebound. We've seen some of our funding sources crumble, learned to work with a new generation of funders who have sharp expectations for our performance, and worked diligently to position ourselves as an ongoing attractive investment. And all of this against a backdrop of terrorism that has chipped away at America's perennial optimism.

Each year is a new year, however. And we console ourselves annually by thinking of how we'll do things in a better or wiser way. But instead of making New Year's resolutions (which you'll break or forget by February), the key to success is to *be resolute* all year long.

Here are a number of ways to bolster your resolve.

Think abundance, not scarcity.

It's easy to fall into the trap of thinking "poor me" when you look at your budget or balance sheet and see the erosion of income or assets. The problem with most of us is that we spend more time looking in mirrors than we do looking through windows.

Think about what you've accomplished over the years in your community. Think about the donors who have helped you. Let them know the residual impact of their investment is strong, and that you're still doing worthy things in spite of the trimming you've had to do.

When we lead from abundance, we can create more abundance. When we lead from scarcity, we remind others of their own scarcity. Convey impact, not need. Putting away the tin cup was something we (hopefully) did years ago.

Subvert mediocrity.

Those who have led great missions – from Clara Barton to Susan B. Anthony to Franklin Roosevelt – were intolerant of mediocrity. While their style for dealing with it may have varied, the end result was the same: they so inspired people with their vision and focus that any latent mediocrity was quelled.

Whether looking at board or staff goals, this is a time for zero tolerance of mediocrity. This is a time for thinking without boundaries and for looking at new ways of getting the job done – through collaborations, partnerships, shifts in staffing, renewal of the board.

Mediocrity weighs an organization down and hampers our ability to serve those who need to be served. Focus on mission – the need you're meeting – and on leadership that encourages excellence.

Position yourself for charitable investment, but don't call yourself a charity.

What's the difference? Plenty. In most people's minds, a charity is an organization that's needy. A charitable *investment*, on the other hand, is a social investment guided by values and a belief in the organization's ability to act on those values in a way that'll satisfy the intent of the donor.

Although *The New York Times* and even publications in our field persist in calling us charities, investors honestly don't think of us that way. They think of us as nonprofits. They see us as an effective third sector, with government and corporations, in addressing the needs of a complex society.

So, check your materials – including your mailings and brochures and website – and make sure you're positioning yourself as a charitable investment. It'll be a significant factor in your success.

Build partnerships, not silos.

The work we do is unceasing, the needs we're meeting keep growing. Other organizations in our communities may have the same or similar missions. It only makes sense to build partnerships with them.

Let donors know you're working together. Ease your contributors' minds about redundancy and overlap, so they know their investment in the issues important to them is being used in the most judicious way for the greatest possible impact.

If you fear another organization eroding your market share, then you're thinking more about your organization than your mission. This isn't a time for silo construction – it's a time for realizing that diminished resources can make a bigger difference when people work together to economize on service delivery and extend their reach to a larger client base.

Keep your investors informed.

Good news, bad news – it makes no difference. Investors want to know what's happening. It's startling how many organizations still resist regular communication with their investors.

Whether you use email, or the telephone, or your newsletter, let your donors know when something of importance happens, whether it's good news (a scholarship made possible by the donor has been awarded) or bad news (a much-sought grant was denied and your programming or services will be affected). Informed investors will keep investing.

Do something new.

Sometimes the best way to energize people and inspire them to reinvest is to break away from business as usual. For example, involve your board in helping to design a new program or exhibition or installation, letting them work with the professionals to see how it's done. Instead of the usual board retreat, do something that's both mental *and* physical – a hike, ropes course, building project, or community service project.

Everyone admires how Habitat for Humanity coalesces its boards, volunteers, and community through building a house. Look for something that'll instill the same camaraderie in your board.

Combat fear.

Fear has swept our world. The media stokes our anxiety daily, and the sizable government investment in combating terrorism is dual edged: it increases our fear while increasing our safety.

What can you do as an organization to help people suppress fear in favor of optimism? Think and talk about success: how you've changed lives, made a difference, or forged new alliances to successfully meet needs.

Master the stories of your success, making them personal and heartwarming. Remind people of the importance of a healthy local community even in a time when we're thinking about a grave global issue. Fear makes our hearts cold; stories of lives touched in positive ways warms them.

Keep your confidence up.

Easy to say, but not easy to do. Still, we have much to be confident about.

Our sector does so much for so many. Our profession is growing and extending its reach. Our volunteer corps is growing – with new faces, new skills, new expectations but with the same dedication to service that's characterized volunteers in this country since the beginning. DeToqueville would still recognize us.

We can also have confidence in ourselves as individuals: confidence we're doing the right thing, making a difference and utilizing vision, mission, and values to engage people as donors and volunteers who'll find great rewards in a time of great stress by getting involved with us.

Be patient, but persistent.

This is a time for patience with the things we can't control (economy, terrorism) and patience with our donors (who are feeling a loss of control as well). We must let them know that investment in our organizations is about the future, that we're in this for the long haul.

We cannot succumb to the corporate measurement standard of one quarter at a time: we have to look backward and forward and see the distance we've come and the distance still to go.

But patience must be accompanied by persistence (lest your very existence and the people you serve be jeopardized). Go back to funders who have turned you down and find out what you can do to earn their support. And keep stewarding donors whose giving has diminished or stopped. They'll come back.

Keep driving towards the light.

My great-grandfather was a visionary man. A rancher, California pioneer, and sage, his philosophy – which he passed along to my grandfather who in turn passed it along to my mother who gave it to me – was to keep driving towards the light. To him, the light represented hope and the future and, as a pioneer often charting his own path, it was a very real orientation point as well.

In my view, it's a good philosophy for us to adopt. Be resolute about driving towards the light. It will move your organization forward, and allow you to fulfill your dreams of what you know you want to accomplish.

Part Two

BOARD AND ORGANIZATIONAL DEVELOPMENT

29

Recruiting and Enlisting the Best Board Possible

Every nonprofit organization dreams of recruiting and retaining a board of visionary planners, generous investors, willing askers, and passionate pragmatists.

Despite those yearnings, too many boards are assembled without a strategy. Board selection is pushed by a date when "a slate" must be presented. Frenzied phone calls result in the inappropriate recruitment of people who may be well-intentioned, but who aren't able to propel the organization to the next level.

Those recruited in haste are often assured that there's "nothing to it" (being on the board, that is). They're told such things as, "You don't have to do anything but come to meetings," or "We just need your name," or (the worst), "We're desperate to submit a full slate of board nominees – please say yes."

Here's what you should know about identifying, recruiting, and retaining a top quality board.

Rebalance the recruitment equation.

Traditional recruitment practices have the same flaw as

traditional fundraising practices: they position the organization's needs ahead of those of the community or prospective board member.

Just as we fund-raise out of desperation until we fully understand it's an investment process based in values and filled with opportunity, we frequently recruit out of desperation until we grasp that board development is also an investment process. Rebalancing the equation requires us to change our strategy.

In many cases what's needed is a new and positive attitude about the recruitment process. For starters, don't assume that people *won't* want to serve; make them feel as though it's a worthy opportunity to serve their community and work with people who share their values.

Don't minimize the seriousness of being a board member. Approach candidates with the attitude that it's a serious undertaking from which they'll benefit greatly.

And don't minimize the commitment. Set standards for board performance. Let people know that yours is an organization that values its volunteers and expects them to give their time, their expertise, and their financial support.

Develop a board recruitment matrix, based on your institutional plan.

In your institutional plan (and here I'll assume there is one) you have focused areas in development, marketing, program, stewardship, and outreach. To fulfill the goals and objectives of your plan, you'll need board members with special skills and connections.

Profile your existing board, assessing such areas as expertise, willingness to ask, linkages in the community, knowledge of your mission and purpose.

You may also want to profile by age, race, geography, gender, and other indicators that are often important to funders when assessing how well your board reflects your community or constituency.

With the profile, or matrix, of the existing board complete, compare it to the needs revealed in your institutional plan. This becomes the tool for recruiting new board members and will help ensure a board that supports organizational development.

Dissolve the Nominating Committee and replace it with a Board Development Committee.

A Board Development Committee or Committee on Trustees has a much larger mandate than simply nominating new board members. It is responsible for recruiting, cultivating, enlisting, orienting, and (heaven forbid!) de-enlisting if board members don't meet the basic requirements of board membership.

This committee develops the board member handbook, conducts the orientation, and is committed to keeping a "stable" of ready recruits at all times.

Unlike a Nominating Committee, which meets just before the slate of candidates is due, the Board Development Committee meets at least quarterly, reviewing prospects and bringing names and profiles to the board for its review all year round.

Prepare and approve a board member job description.

There are many models for board member job descriptions. The key criterion is clarity.

Specifically, be sure to state expectations regarding financial support, attendance at meetings, committee membership, attendance at events, fiscal and legal responsibility, evaluation of executive director, and other related functions.

In addition, add some expectations that are more attitudinal than performance-based: loyalty in time of crisis, willingness to communicate concerns through appropriate channels, respect

213

for staff, and willingness to use appropriate avenues for approaching staff. Unless stated, any of these can become difficult issues in times of crisis or transition.

Do "prospecting" for board members, using the board matrix.

Just as you gather names of prospective donors from board members and the community, do the same for generating names of potential board members. Some boards do this, but it tends to be a random process. Have board members bring one name to each board meeting. Have senior staff members do the same. Once you've given the Board Development Committee the names, they should use the same process used for developing fundraising prospect lists.

They qualify the names by contacting the individual who suggested the name, getting as much information as possible; they develop a strategy for recruitment; and they cultivate the prospective board member with lunch meetings, tours, and other opportunities to meet people and learn more about the organization.

Some potential candidates may instead want to serve on committees. This is a great proving ground, and allows both candidate and organization to learn if there's a fit.

At a certain point in the developing relationship, you'll know if this is a potential board member. If there's a good match, and if there's an appropriate opening, you can enlist. If there's not an opening, you'll need to keep the candidate involved and interested until such time.

In your recruitment and enlistment, don't focus only on the expertise (banking, legal, fundraising, marketing) the new board member will bring to the organization.

214

Focus also on the mission, vision, and values of the organization. Your goal is to have passionate pragmatists on your board. Without passion, advocacy is often minimal. Remember that there are two bottom lines for nonprofits: the values return, and the financial stability. Passionate pragmatists understand both.

A board that thrives is one that is truly involved.

Active involvement in committees and activities is an obvious responsibility, but there's also participation in decision-making and policy-making.

Sometimes strong executive directors with strong executive committees want to make all the decisions and create all the policies, using the board as a rubber stamp. This is the quickest way to lose good board members.

On one board, an individual with a great deal to offer became so frustrated that she resigned after three meetings. Basically, she said there was nothing to do, as everything was predetermined before the meeting. Although involved on a committee, it wasn't enough. She wanted to be part of the discussions and decisions around issues.

Board meetings must be relevant, interesting, marked by dialogue and discussion, and should never be a waste of time.

Publish a board calendar at the beginning of the year. Make sure the meeting dates are easy to track (second Tuesday of every other month, for instance) and that the calendar is maintained except in emergencies.

Construct agenda that include a "mission moment" (a testimonial or presentation in the middle of the session by a client or community resident who's benefited from your work).

Devote time at each meeting to an issue of importance, not just to committee reports and other predictable agenda items. Promote dialogue and discussion. And do your best to control those who would dominate.

Celebrate your board and let them get to know each other (if they choose) outside of board meetings.

Those who come together to decide the future and fate of our nonprofits have agreed to an important responsibility. The meetings have a serious purpose. But injecting warmth and humor into the board meetings can go a long way.

Consider an annual retreat, where there's time for casual interaction and even some planned activities to help board members get to know each other. Have an award that's given to board members that has a bit of whimsy attached.

One board, which had undergone a considerable growth transition (from five to 15 members) and was trying diligently to become more committed, dreamed up the following award. They were discussing the difference between involvement and commitment, and were told by a facilitator that the difference was best illustrated by consideration of a breakfast of ham and eggs. In that breakfast, the chicken was involved, but the pig was committed.

The board members decided to give the "Pig Award" at each meeting to the board member who had shown the most commitment. And so it began: a Miss Piggy magnet circulated from refrigerators to filing cabinets for years, reminding each month's winner that others were grateful for their commitment.

Social events for board members can also be held, but remember not all board members will care to participate. The purpose is to bring board members closer together so they'll understand the texture and dynamics of themselves as a board and be able to reach decisions more effectively.

216

•••

Board members are an organization's major investors, regardless of the size of the gift they make. The time, effort and advocacy they give, in addition to their gifts, have a huge impact on the overall health and community perception of the organization. When recruited and enlisted appropriately, and involved and engaged during their board service, they will thrive. And so will your organization.

30

What to Ask Every Prospective Board Member

Often, in our haste to meet a deadline for recruiting board members, we whisk through the interview process or forego it entirely, relying on what we know about individuals through other connections or word of mouth information about them.

Even when we do a proper interview, we tend to focus only on the obvious – expertise, experience, interest in serving on the board. We don't dig deep enough into areas that in the long run are far better indicators of successful board service.

Here are some questions you may not have thought to ask. They will reveal things that can be important to your organization as you build a relationship that you hope will be durable, motivating, and productive.

How passionate are you about our cause?

Passion is the driver when it comes to asking others for money, being an ambassador in the community, or being an effective advocate. In attempting to fill out a recruitment matrix (banker, corporate vice president, community volunteer) we shouldn't overlook the passion dimension.

One arts organization, in its quest to form a more "corporate board," recruited a number of business superstars but failed to test for passion. Little money was raised other than what came by courtesy from the member's corporations. There was little participation at concerts and events. And ultimately some decisions were made that were harmful to the organization. Why? Because the passion factor was lacking.

How much time can you give to us?

This is critical. To slide over this question, hoping the individual, when confirmed, will make time when we need it is unrealistic. One university, when enlisting volunteers for a capital campaign, was savvy enough to put the time requirement at the bottom of every volunteer job description. When volunteers committed to the job, they knew it would take (for example) two hours a week.

While some board members may be enlisted because they offer a connection or a presence that could be more important than time, most board members are enlisted to serve. And serving requires time.

Setting time standards is one of the ways we convey the importance of our organization to volunteers.

What motivates you as a volunteer?

This is an important question to ask in initial conversations. You want to know what will keep this person engaged over the years.

The best answer will come when you query the candidate about their previous board or volunteer service. Which organizations provided the environment in which the volunteer flourished, and which did not?

A direct question about what motivates a candidate can also work, but not as effectively.

You're trying to match board nominees to the culture and practices of your organization – be sure yours is an environment in which the candidate will be motivated.

What expectations do you have from the management of organizations on whose boards you serve?

This, too, is important to know. We evaluate each other and organizations on expectations we sometimes fail to communicate. These expectations can be as granular as wanting to receive board materials at least a week before meetings or as global as only serving on boards of financially stable organizations.

If the person's expectations are unrealistic or don't align with where your organization is at present (for example, you're dragging around a $700,000 accumulated deficit), then it's better to find that out in the recruitment process.

In your enlistment conversation, you can, for instance, be candid with the candidate about the deficit, why it exists and your plans to eliminate it, and let him decide whether he wants to serve.

What are your personal dreams or aspirations that could be enhanced by service on our board?

Younger board members often view board service as a way not only to serve, but to gain connections and experience to advance their careers. Similarly, there are individuals seeking board positions who are looking to make career changes, acquire new skills, or learn more about the nonprofit sector.

To meet these needs, you must first uncover what they are.

But, as importantly, you must keep them at the front of your mind during the board member's term of service. In this way, you'll encourage people's growth and participation in our sector or give the board members experiences (marketing, writing, speaking) that will advance their careers. You set up a win/win situation, and deepen the board member's commitment to and appreciation for the organization.

What professional or personal constraints on your time or service might you anticipate?

The people we want are often the same people everyone else wants to recruit. They may already serve on other boards or have demanding high-profile jobs. In addition to the time constraints, this creates attention constraints.

In one organization, the co-chair of the development committee was asked by a second organization on whose board he served to chair its endowment campaign. Although he had plenty of time to give, it was soon apparent that the endowment campaign was getting much more of his attention and energy. The first organization found itself without his previously significant involvement.

An in-demand board candidate should be candid about where your organization fits among his philanthropic priorities, and whether being chair of another organization's board or project will be too distracting.

Your choice, then, is to enlist anyway, in the hope you'll gain his attention, or to delay enlisting until a future time in which the candidate will have your organization as a higher priority.

Are you willing to make a financial commitment that is a stretch?

We are getting better at putting this question on the table, but still we falter. We have to be upfront about our expectations of a board member's financial commitment. As with time, financial support is an expectation we need to communicate clearly.

While I'm not an advocate of a "minimum board gift" (believing we not only drive off people who can't give the minimum but allow those who could give more to give less), I am a firm advocate of 100 percent board giving at a level that is a stretch.

What is a stretch? It is a gift that is larger than a person might otherwise give. Let people know at the outset that you expect them to give at this level. If they use the "time is money" response, reconsider their suitability as a board member.

Of what importance to you is social interaction with other board members?

Some boards have a culture that encourages frequent opportunities for social interaction; other boards see this as unimportant. This is another aspect of the "match."

A board recruit may barely have time to come to meetings and serve on a committee or two, let alone feel obligated to socialize. When a person doesn't want to mix philanthropic service with her social life, it can create an awkward situation with other board members.

A person who fails to attend board social events may never be fully embraced by the other board members. Likewise, if a person is seeking not only a volunteer experience but a social experience, and your board's culture is not social, there may be a problem.

How do you feel about performance evaluations of individual board members and boards as a group?

Individual member and full board performance evaluations

have become more routine. Experienced board members may expect an evaluation or may feel that it's useless, a waste of time, or inappropriate.

Explore their knowledge of the process, and listen for potential objections if your practice is to evaluate formally on an annual or biannual basis. Some organizations have adopted the practice (which I encourage) of having the CEO and the board chair meet annually with each board member to thank them for their service, review their concerns, find out their committee or project preferences, and to ask for their gift.

If this is something you're doing, let each board recruit know during the enlistment process about that annual meeting. That way, he or she won't be surprised when the board chair calls for an appointment.

As you think about the three primary board roles – ambassador, advocate and asker – in which role(s) do you think you'll want to be most active?

This is the "capstone" question – and allows potential board members to see how you've organized board involvement and where they fit in. It opens their imagination to ways they can serve that fit their own goals and motivations and best utilize their experience and community contacts.

With this delineation, you offer many ways to get involved, though of course it's always good to say that the goal is for board members to fulfill all three roles!

•••

These questions should give you a much more detailed profile of your board recruit, and provide better information on which to build a productive and mutually fulfilling relationship.

Like hiring an employee, we need to get beyond the obvious information and find out what really motivates a potential board member. Then our job is to make sure we remember these motivations as we assign, coach, and reward board members.

31

What to Ask Before Joining a Board of Directors

"The call has come. You've been asked to serve on a nonprofit board. You have mixed feelings.

If you're new to boards, you may be anxious about your responsibilities and what's expected of you, while feeling pride and a certain sense of accomplishment that you've been selected.

"If you're an experienced board member, willing to be called into service again, you may have feelings of renewed pride, or even joy, and may be thinking, 'This is the board I've been waiting to serve on!'"

–*From the Introduction to The Ultimate Board*
Member's Book, by Kay Sprinkel Grace, Emerson &
Church, Publishers

Knowing we shouldn't enter into board roles "lightly or unadvisedly," and that the commitment is intended to last at least through several consecutive terms, it's prudent to ask some hard questions of the organization wanting to enlist you.

Let me assume you've already explored areas like mission, vision, and values and that you fully endorse these. What I'll discuss below are the "drill down" questions that can make the difference between an enlightened enlistment and a difficult adjustment.

Job description.

Hopefully, you'll be presented with a job description when recruited. You'll be asked to review it, and then during a later meeting have a chance to ask specific questions about the various responsibilities and expectations listed.

If you're not given a job description to review, then your first question is: "May I see a job description for board members and one for the committee(s) on which you think I might be interested in serving?"

If the organization cannot provide these descriptions, you can hope they go back to the office and write them very quickly. Don't enlist unless you see it in writing.

It's about time.

This is the next biggest question: "How much time do you expect me to give each month?" Ask the organization's recruiters to be absolutely honest. You would rather have it overestimated than underestimated.

Often in their eagerness to recruit busy people with high visibility, organizations understate the time expectation. Press for details. How many meetings? What responsibilities outside of meetings?

One successful recruiter of extremely busy people stated the amount of time required at the bottom of the board member job description – and also on the committee job descriptions.

This spared new board members the unpleasant surprise of

finding that what was represented as "one meeting every other month" turned out to be approximately five hours a month in other required activities.

Show me the money.

Many boards have a minimum gift requirement; others have a "give or get" expectation. Find out what your board expects. Determine whether it's a level you can or want to give. And certainly expect to be asked to give at a stretch level.

Increasingly, outside funders gauge their willingness to give by the aggregate amount of board giving – and 100 percent board participation in annual and campaign giving is no longer a dream, it's a standard.

You need to ask, "What is your expectation of what I should give, when do you expect that gift, and do I have to give all of it or can I, for example, get my employer to match my gift to reach the full amount?"

Party time.

One concern board members have expressed to me repeatedly is the feeling of being "nickel and dimed" once they get on a board. Even if they've settled on the size and timing of their gift, they find they're often sideswiped by the sudden admonition that there's a $500 per couple dinner, or an auction at which they're expected to buy merchandise, or other event that will add to their overall financial commitment.

Ask the question when you explore the board gift: "In addition to my board gift, what other expectations do you have regarding support for ongoing special events or activities?" That way, there are no surprises.

Role fulfillment.

In addition to the job description, there may be expectations because of a particular skill or expertise you have (banking, marketing, fundraising, public relations). Determine if this is the role the organization sees you playing, and how that'll be reflected in your assignments.

Ask, "I have reviewed the job description and it seems reasonable. But, since I suspect I've been recruited because of my fundraising experience, what roles beyond this job description do you see me playing?"

The dialogue that comes from this question can offer you opportunities to explain any other fundraising you're doing, and determine whether it would represent a conflict of interest.

Getting to know you.

Before you sign up for a board, it's wise to meet as many of the board members as possible and to meet key staff people with whom you may be working (for example, if you're coming in to offer fundraising expertise, you should meet the development staff).

Chemistry plays a role in successful relationships of all kinds. Board membership is no different. Your question, before you say yes, might be: "I'm happy to consider joining your board, but before I do I'd appreciate an opportunity to sit in on a meeting and would like to meet some of the staff I'd be working with. Is that possible?"

If it's not possible, pass on the opportunity. It's probably a closed culture you might not enjoy. Most organizations would jump at the chance, considering it an indication of thoughtful analysis regarding your fit with the board and the organization.

The numbers game.

It goes without saying that you need to check the financial information before joining the board. You have fiscal and legal responsibility as a trustee, and it's important to know the fiscal viability of the organization before you join. Sadly, some organizations still struggle with true transparency in reporting. Now, however, Congress and some states have tightened the requirements and are making accountability their business as well as ours.

As a potential board member, ask the enlisting team: "May I see your audited financial statements for the past several years, and a copy of your current budget and balance sheet? I'd also appreciate the chance to talk with your CFO (if there is one) or CEO after I have had a chance to review the information."

Ignorance is no excuse when it comes to accountability.

Friend and fundraising.

Even if you weren't recruited because of your fundraising expertise, you'll still be asked to participate in the donor development process including identifying, helping to qualify, and cultivating potential donors to the organization.

Find out exactly what is expected of you: "Who is responsible for directly asking for money, and what kinds of activities do you expect board members to get involved in?"

Get a good sense of what's expected – list review, individual meetings to review strategy, signing letters, making phone calls, participating in thankathons – these can add to the time commitment in ways that may not have been factored in.

Separation of powers.

Find out what the rules are before you join. What are staff

responsibilities? What are board responsibilities? While the pat answer for decades has been, "Board sets policy and staff carries it out," we know that the "blur" has been creeping.

Identify several areas – for example, finance, fundraising, program, marketing – and for each one ask, "Typically, what roles do board members play in this area and what powers and responsibilities are reserved to staff?"

This could be telling, and could reveal some murkiness about responsibilities and perhaps some areas of staff weakness or creeping micromanagement by the board.

Evaluation.

There are two areas of evaluation you need to explore: "What is the process for evaluating the CEO?" and "How does the board evaluate its own performance?"

Evaluation – particularly in an environment of increased accountability from government and funders – is critical. A board with a formal process for CEO evaluation and board self-evaluation is a board that's already aware of what the future will require. These are assuring signals. If neither of these functions are well managed on a regular basis, it could be a signal of deeper disorganization and lack of accountability.

•••

When you ask questions such as these, members of the board you're joining will realize they have a thinking and committed candidate before them. But the benefit is yours, too. You'll know that you will have explored some of the most potentially troublesome areas for board member satisfaction and received answers that have increased your willingness to lend your time, expertise, and resources to this organization.

As I wrote in the conclusion of *The Ultimate Board*

Member's Book:

"When the call for board service comes, seize the opportunity ... Answer the call, spread your wings, do your best, understand and respect the sector, and champion the organization."

But, ask these questions, first!

32

Recruiting Younger People For Your Board

Let's face it. None of us is getting any younger. And, when you look around the boardroom table, that fact becomes alarmingly clear.

When we consider the number of younger people – those in their 20s, 30s and 40s – who stepped forward as volunteers or donor-investors during the roaring 1990s economy, we should now see a proportionate number involved as board members or as committee or task force members. We should, but we don't. These younger investors aren't involved in any great numbers with governance, policy, and planning.

We know we need young people to infuse our organizations with ideas, energy, and a new generation of connections. After all, the recruitment matrix for most nonprofit boards calls for diversity of race, ethnicity, geography, skills, expertise, and age. But, of all of those vectors, the one still ignored the most is age.

The dilemma has two dimensions. In perpetuating their boards, board members seek those like themselves – in general, people in their 50s, 60s, and 70s. Some board members, as well, say they don't know where to look for younger members, which often is just an excuse.

However, there is another reason why younger people aren't on boards in the numbers they should be. When observing or interacting with boards at events or occasional meetings, younger people often don't like what they see – namely "bored" meetings in which politics and power issues, endless discussions, and a focus on "administrivia" lead them to feel negatively about board service.

How can we successfully recruit younger people to our boards? First, by opening our minds and eyes to the talents they bring and then by reaching out in entirely new recruitment arenas and engaging them.

But second, by ensuring that what they would find when joining our boards is what they're looking for.

Here's what you should know about what younger people are looking for in an organization.

Focus.

Youth has always been impatient, but this is a more impatient generation than most boards are used to. As a result, it's important to stay focused yet responsive in board meeting discussions.

Run your board meetings well. Have a mission and vision that are evident, and tasks supporting them that are well organized, assigned, and evaluated.

Confine board discussions to the key points that need to be reviewed to make a decision – leave deeper explorations of issues and nuances to committee meetings and bring the essence to the board.

Otherwise, you'll lose the attention and interest of this younger generation who may process things more quickly or

233

bring a different style of analysis to the table.

Relevance.

This is key. Your organization's mission – as the expression of why you exist – must be relevant to the community needs you're meeting. Derived from that, your programs and actions must be relevant, too.

Younger board members may need additional information to connect your organization and its impact to something relevant in their lives. It may be hard for a Gen-X person, seated on the board of an agency dealing with the needs of the aging, to identify with those needs. Tours and conversations with clients and hard data about the growth in numbers of people in your community over 60 (and over 85!) will help younger members understand the economic and social impact of your programs.

Action.

Nonprofits are change agents and yet, as I've written before in this book, we're often reluctant to change. We hide behind dialogue and deliberation, and sometimes delay implementation beyond the tolerance of our donors or the needs of the community.

Younger people are looking for action, not talk. Many feel we've talked some issues into inertia without solving them. They seek participation in actions to correct, address, or solve the problems that have been around for their entire lives. In short, they want to get on with it.

Impact.

Younger people are looking for measurable impact of their financial and time involvement. They want to know how many people you're serving, how many are attending the concert, or how many signed up for the run. Then, they want to know how much money you raised, how it'll be spent, and what difference will be made by that investment.

Tell them the statistics, but enlarge their understanding of the sector by telling them stories, too. Let them meet people who have benefited from their investment. Engage them in backstage or behind the scenes opportunities with performing and visual arts – and let them see, as well, the impact you're having on school children, seniors, or others you serve.

Having program staff describe the impact isn't good enough – you need to let board members (of all ages) see it, hear it, and know it from those who have directly or indirectly benefited from your work.

Involvement.

The desire of younger investors to be involved with the programs in which they have invested is keen.

Young people, working together in local organizations, have for several generations made an impact on our communities. They volunteer in hospitals, in summer camps, with seniors and the disabled, and behind the scenes in the performing and visual arts.

Why should they have to stop this direct involvement when they reach the age and station in life when they're considered for board service? Sitting at a boardroom table once a month, or six times yearly, cannot and should not substitute for hands-on experience with the programs themselves.

Connections.

One reason younger people come on the board is the same reason older people do: to be with others who share their values and interests. But with younger people there's an added reason – they can operate as peers with people who by reason of profession or reputation are vastly senior to them.

This is a wonderful opportunity to work with and observe people who become role models for them in both their board work and their professional lives. It is a true "perk" that becomes quite appealing to younger people in the recruitment process.

Fun.

Let's not forget this. Younger people want to have fun when they give their time to an organization or cause. Be sure your board knows how to have fun – not just at parties, but at the board meetings as well. A humorless board meeting is a terrible experience for anyone.

Admittedly, if the business of the meeting is grim or very serious, you cannot focus on fun. But for the most part we take board business entirely too seriously – failing to see that even if our work is serious, we don't need to banish laughter or lightness from the boardroom (see chapter on board meetings).

Many a difficult issue has been resolved when someone had the courage to see the humor, irony, or absurdity of the situation.

Growth.

As just mentioned, the opportunity to work with those who are senior to them is a tremendous source of growth for many younger people.

When setting up "buddies" or mentors, link younger board members with more senior ones from whom they can learn not only about your organization, but about skills or professions that may be similar to their ambitions.

In your formation of committees or task forces, find out from these younger members what skills they bring and what they would like to learn.

Finally, in your board meetings, follow good board procedures and practices such as formal agendas, appropriate committee reports (not too long, focused on action), courtesy in dealing with divergent opinions, time limits on discussion, and dealing with critical issues openly. This will give younger board members a solid foundation in what you hope will be a lifetime of service to the nonprofit sector.

Leverage.

Let younger people see that their board service can be leverage in their lives. While the time they spend with your organization will detract from the hours they may have for other pursuits, they should realize that this experience gives them a new circle of people with whom to build relationships now and in the future.

Their role in fundraising and other community outreach will provide connections and visibility that can be an enhancement to their own personal goals. And the connections they bring – with the next generation – can only better leverage the future of the organization.

Skills.

People of all ages bring skills and learn skills when they're on a board. It's too easy to think younger people stand more to gain than give.

Young people bring ease with technology, agility at problem solving, understanding about what marketing is effective with their own age group, innovative approaches to problems that have challenged us older folks for years, and other skills that we must fathom and savor and appreciate.

We can learn much from them, and they from us. Having

younger people on board can result in mutual skill sharpening and sharing.

•••

Reducing the average age of your board by getting younger people on it is a worthy idea. If you've hesitated to expand your matrix, or haven't assessed how appealing your board would be to younger members, now may be just the time.

33

Working with the New Generation Of Board Members

A new generation of board members has arrived. We wanted them. We searched for them. We recruited and enlisted them. And now in many organizations we're wondering what to do with them.

Impatient, bottom-line oriented, inexperienced with nonprofit boards yet wanting to make a difference in their communities – these men and women bring energy, a new dynamic, and are disrupting the status quo at organizations throughout America.

Younger Baby Boomers (those just past 40) and Generation X'ers defy categorization except to say they bring a leadership style that's sometimes confrontational, ask questions that are deeply probing, and want our organizations to operate more like businesses.

So what can we do with this new crop of potential board members who need understanding and guidance about the sector if they, and we, are going to have a productive relationship?

Here is what's important to know to bring these new board members along at your organization.

Conduct an orientation that's not only an overview of your organization, but also an introduction to how the sector works.

So many of the "new philanthropists" who emerged in the 90s are now board members. And while they believe in the sector's impact on the community, they're often unschooled in how we work.

Let these new recruits know how much the sector raises each year in America. Explain to them the idea of "holding an organization in trust," and how that charge requires (sometimes slow and cumbersome) consensus decision-making.

Remind them that a public benefit corporation uses other people's money to do its work and is therefore accountable to donors. Most of the newer board members are well aware of Sarbanes-Oxley, but few may know about the similar obligation to donors.

Be sure their recruitment is based on shared vision and values, and an understanding of the mission.

Sometimes in our zeal to recruit the rising star from the local technology company, we focus on the skill-set and connections they bring, not on their understanding or support for our mission, vision, and values.

Even if they're the best marketing, accounting, legal, or other minds of their generation, if they don't know and share your vision and values, they'll have a short life on your board.

It is the "soft stuff" that keeps the wind in people's sails – it's what empowers them to ask for money, serve as ambassadors for your organization, and as formal or informal advocates.

One arts board, which had evolved from a group of people passionate about music into a board of corporate and professional people with little or no experience (or taste) for music, nearly stripped the organization of its key education program. Their rationale, it was a "loss leader" so needed to be cut.

Avoid this by emphasizing your organization's core values, vision, and mission when recruiting.

Be clear about your expectations.

Eager to get to yes, we sometimes slide by board responsibilities such as giving, serving on committees, or attending events. In doing so, we downgrade the importance of board service.

For some of your recruits, this will be their first nonprofit board. You will set the standard. Be specific about what you expect. More than their mothers or fathers, these individuals expect to see a job description and know the requirements before signing on.

Time is our most precious commodity – especially with young people juggling jobs, families, and aspirations. Tell them directly what you expect and how much time it will take. If they can't make that commitment, then suggest service on a committee or task force, rather than the board, until they have more time to offer.

Be willing to adapt your communication style to theirs.

The email world we live in has created expectations about instant and timely communications and the format and style of these communications. I've watched as well-intentioned staff pass out reams of paper at a board meeting and have heard newer board members (who often bring their Wi-Fi equipped laptops to meetings) say, "Why didn't you just email this to me – I hate paper."

Communications are different today. We operate in a world of "tight one-pagers" and bullet point reports. Our long narratives, while serving us in the past, may not be what these newer board members are expecting or want.

This is particularly true with strategic plans. As someone who was trained and seasoned in an era of narrative plans, I personally have had to adjust to the format that this newer generation prefers. It doesn't change the content; just the way it's presented.

Find out what motivates them and lead to that motivation.

Baby Boomers and Gen X'ers have spent considerably more time than their parents and grandparents figuring out who they are. They know what they want and don't want to do. Many of them have changed careers and jobs several times already and aren't done yet.

Most bring myriad skills and varied experience – your challenge is to determine where to deploy their already-honed interests. Identify at the outset what inspires them to work hard: doing things on their own (projects), with others (on a standing committee or strategic task force), or serving in an advisory capacity (audit or investment committee).

If you haven't already begun annual individual meetings with all board members to determine how they can best serve the organization, now is a good time to begin. You'll be delighted with the range of ideas that emerges.

Analyze your board meetings and make sure they're productive, interesting, and inspiring.

You can do everything I've said above, and if your board meetings are deadly, the new generation won't stay with you. And, if you block their suggestions or fail to think how your board meetings could be more lively and interesting, word will get around and you'll have trouble recruiting other younger people.

Limit committee and staff reports. Start and end on time. Have a crisp agenda. Select an issue for discussion at every board meeting – something pithy and germane to the community or the organization. Have a "mission moment" where a client (or client's family) or a member of the dance company or orchestra, talks to the board about just how important the board's work is.

Inspire them. Grow them. Don't bore them. And, if it's a budget meeting or some other potentially difficult session, make sure the information is accurate, provided in advance, and that the discussion is managed in a productive way.

Convey to them what the board culture of your organization is like.

I've been to a number of board meetings lately where some of the young and restless members bordered on being inappropriate in their dialogue with the CEO or another board member. Budgeting and strategic planning seem to raise these flash points considerably.

This behavior is sometimes a reflection of how the new generation operates within their companies. I remember someone describing Intel years ago in a book for college graduates. The plus side was the intellectual stimulation and a great product; the minus was, "They yell at each other a lot."

If that isn't your culture, don't tolerate it. Snip it off at first bud. Not in front of the board, but in a follow up meeting or phone call.

Be open to new ways of planning, budgeting, or fundraising that they may suggest.

Younger people were raised in a marketing environment that was flooded with many more messages than in previous decades. They are savvy and know what works. They know how they like to be asked for a gift, and what they like to read and hear about an organization. They know what works for them and for their contemporaries. And they are your new market.

Team them up with a continuing board member – someone more traditional – so they have a "buddy" for the first year or so.

You don't have to call it a "buddy system" – that's not appealing to lots of people. But find some way of teaming new board members with more experienced ones to learn the culture, the ropes, the organization, and find out how they can adapt their energy and motivation in the most productive way possible.

Even the most confident young person can feel alone when entering a room filled with strangers who are older. Which is another point: when recruiting your first younger board members, try to recruit two or three at the same time. They'll enjoy the company.

Do deliberate team-building with the board as new people are introduced, to ensure greater tolerance and better interaction.

None of this should be left to chance. We need to be strategic about building the future of our organizations, and these young people are our future. If at all possible, have a board retreat soon after new recruits come on board. Include intentional team-building activities as well as issue-focused provocative conversation.

Diversity on boards isn't just gender, age, racial or ethnic – it is diversity of decision-making styles, experience, and skills. The lens through which we focus this is the shared vision and values, and the commitment to mission

•••

Younger board members. You need them. You want them. And by heeding some of the suggestions here you can offer them an experience they've never had before – one that expands their skills and their vision for your community ... while greatly benefiting your organization along the way.

34

Developing a Board of Champions

I suspect it was some 1950s ad for Charles Atlas body building lessons ("Don't be a 90 pound weakling") that used the phrase, "Champions are made, not born." That's true in the nonprofit sector as well. Every organization needs champions – men and women who are enthusiastic advocates for its programs and impact.

If your board isn't out there championing your organization, now's the time to put into place some practices that will turn them into unabashed promoters of your work.

Here's what you should know about turning yours into a board of champions.

Be an enthusiast yourself.

Whatever your role – CEO, development director, CFO – be mindful of your own enthusiasm when talking with board members.

Too often we're tempted to take people "into our confidence" and begin pulling somewhat soiled laundry out of the bag. We flavor our comments with an unbecoming cynicism about people, the organization, or the sector. We whine.

Then, we're chagrined when our board members are unwilling to champion us through their roles as ambassadors, askers, and advocates. No surprise.

If staff isn't enthusiastic, how can the board hear and tell the mission, stories, and outcomes with any degree of excitement?

Tell the board the truth – good news or bad news.

It's easier to share good news than bad. But board members need to hear both. Let them decide how bad the news is. Is it an incentive to step out into the community and rally people around a worthy organization that's having a hard time? Or is it the last turn in the shutting off of their faith in you?

Whatever result may occur, you can't withhold bad news. Champions are with you through good times and bad. If you fail to disclose, things will get worse – you can be sure of that.

Tell the board what you want them to do.

Board members want specificity in their assignments. Telling them to go out and champion your organization is like telling them to go out and raise money – but not giving them training, assignments, or someone to partner with on the solicitation.

Be specific in what you want your board members to do. For example, enlist good speakers in a speaker's bureau and get them out to service clubs, churches, youth organizations, or other appropriate venues.

Get reliable correspondents to agree to send out personal notes to individuals whose names and addresses you provide.

Use powerfully connected people to leverage their contacts and your accomplishments into increased recognition or funding.

Give all board members talking points they can use whether on the golf course, during aerobics classes, or at a luncheon. In short, give them championship training.

Give board members opportunities to be champions with your staff.

Regular well-planned and appropriately timed visits to your programs from a small group of board members has a double benefit: the staff feels championed because board members express their appreciation for what staff is doing; and board members become even greater champions (and have more stories to tell) because of the time they spend at your site.

If confidentiality prohibits a visit, arrange for staff to meet with board and tell them (or show a video) about the impact of their work.

Celebrate your champions.

Just as heroes are a key part of corporate culture, so are champions. At board meetings, tell the stories of those who championed your cause at its beginning, during tough passages, or year after year with extraordinary sustained commitment.

Champions inspire champions. Tipping point stories – the quiet moment when things change at last – are often the stories of champions. Use your newsletter, website, email updates and other communications to let people know that yours is an organization that celebrates its champions.

Look for strong values connections in those you recruit for the board.

Temper the process of "functional recruitment" (for example, banker, lawyer, accountant, marketer) by making sure these individuals are in synch with your values. Having a banker isn't enough: you need a banker with an understanding of and passion for your mission and impact.

I've seen some poor decisions made by boards whose functional match was excellent but whose "mission match" was poor. The higher the match between your organization's values and the board member's values, the greater the level of unwavering championship you can count on – even in times of trial.

The care and feeding of champions.

Wheaties may be the breakfast of champions, but mission is the feast. Champions rally because of the way your group meets the needs of the community. Keep defining those needs, and showing how you're meeting them.

And in your board recruitment, enlistment, and orientation, immerse your new candidates in the mission by taking them on tours, having them meet clients (if possible), families of clients, or the organization's program providers.

Connect them with other champions.

Your organization is probably one of several in the community that are concerned with a similar mission (programs for the aging, disabled, families in crisis, music, art, education). These organizations have champions, too.

Collaboration among organizations with similar missions not only makes sense in a crowded nonprofit market, it is increasingly required by funders.

Help your champions become champions not just for you, but for the larger mission as well, by connecting them with other people with the same passion and commitment. It will expand their horizons and give them an even broader playing field on which to excel.

When championship wavers, don't ignore it – find out why.

If someone has been your champion and suddenly (or gradually) wavers, find out why. This may be the canary in the mineshaft: an early warning signal you may not otherwise notice. In one organization, the most dedicated and enthusiastic champions – drawn by the entrepreneurial beginnings and the ground-breaking practices of the early leaders – disengaged when bureaucracy grew and innovation declined.

Organizations change and it won't always be possible to retain all your champions. Still, you'll hold onto more of them if you take the time to learn why their commitment is wavering. There may well be a relatively easy remedy available.

•••

As advocates and ambassadors, champions can help make your organization and your mission more visible and effective. Create champions by engaging board members in ways that give them the feeling of not only being champions, but of playing on a championship team as well.

250

35

Creating Ambassadors Among Your Board

For the past several years, I've been working with organizations to help them implement a "AAA" program to motivate their boards – AAA being shorthand for Ambassador, Advocate and Asker.

The purpose of the program is to allow board members to identify their own motivation and apply it to needed tasks within the organization. It's based on the reality that not all board members are motivated by the same activities, and that while we'd love all board members to be Askers, the truth is that many prefer to be Ambassadors or Advocates instead. The success has been remarkable.

When board members are able to indicate the tasks they want to do, the fulfillment of assignments increases. There's another important outcome as well: as board members flourish in their roles as Ambassadors or Advocates, they find themselves increasingly exposed to willing and interested donors.

After a while, Ambassadors and Advocates become more aware of the desire donors have to give and the joy they derive from it. This realization has helped many an Ambassador and

Advocate become Askers.

Any person who serves on a board should be willing to be an Ambassador. No one is off the hook. Simply stated, an Ambassador makes friends for the organization; an Advocate makes the case, and the Asker makes the ask.

Here's what you should know about creating Ambassadors and what they do.

Present the role of Ambassador as something everyone can do.

Often, we have so elevated the role of asker that people on our boards who simply cannot or will not participate feel as though their service is less appreciated.

By telling board members that Ambassadors make friends and have key outreach roles in cultivating prospective donors and stewarding continuing donor-investors, we dignify and endorse the role.

Be alert for stories in your organization about people who contribute greatly through their cultivation and stewardship efforts.

I often tell the story of the woman who insisted she would do "anything but ask for money." I responded by asking what she would do, and she told me she had great lists. That was an understatement. She not only had great lists – she had made great friends for the organization as well.

This lady was a cultivator and steward and, when her "list" was called on for leadership gifts to a small capital campaign, they gave generously and cited their friend as the reason for giving.

When I told her she had raised $500,000 for the capital campaign, she of course denied it because, "I can't ask for money." My response: "You don't have to. You do such a good job making people love the organization, that it makes it easy for others to ask."

Although being friendly may be second nature, good Ambassadors need to be well oriented.

Being an Ambassador is a serious and important role for board members. When they meet someone who asks about the organization, they need to be well oriented, which means receiving regular updates via email or snail mail.

At board meetings, be sure to include upbeat information about what's going on at your organization, and don't forget the "mission moment" when someone from the community talks about the importance of your work. Provide Ambassadors with "talking points" at least once a quarter.

As part of their training and orientation, make sure Ambassadors are masters of the "elevator speech" (and the "elevator question").

The elevator speech is particularly important for Ambassadors. It is that quick summary of what your organization does, what it stands for, and what its most current activities are.

But it is equally important for Ambassadors to be able to finish their elevator speech with an "elevator question." This may be something like, "You seem interested. Is there other information I can offer?" Or "In what I've just described, is there anything of particular interest to you?" Or "Perhaps you'd like to come for a visit or a tour and see what we're doing first hand?"

Ambassadors are great thankers.

If you're not currently conducting regular "thankathons,"

think about starting one.

Ambassadors are terrific at this task. Although they won't connect with every donor, they can still leave a message. And, those with whom they do connect will reinforce the Ambassador's experience with delighted donors.

One organization has people who come in every other Saturday to telephone members and thank them. Recently, they've begun calling members just prior to the time they receive their annual renewal letter and the renewal rate is increasing.

Ambassadors are usually great party people.

When planning an event, plan the role for your Ambassadors. Be sure they have a list of people you'd like them to talk with. Give them some background on each. And provide a special designation for Ambassadors, an "Ask Me" button is a good idea at a large event.

Ambassadors should circulate among the guests and provide welcoming words, directions or enough conversation to make people feel at home and to find out what some of their interests are.

Ambassadors need to know what to do with the information they uncover.

Let Ambassadors know that you'll want a "brain dump" from them after the event. Set up a template on your website, or simply encourage them to send an email. If they don't use email, offer a form to fill out that they can fax to you. Or, just make sure you, or volunteers working with you, do a "call down" within a day or so to get the news while it's fresh.

Whatever method you use, your goal is to record who the Ambassadors talked with, what they talked about, were there questions they couldn't answer, what information would the person like, and what other follow-up might be needed.

Be specific in the tasks you offer to Ambassadors.

Provide a checklist when you meet with Ambassadors to discern their interest in development activities. In organizations in which I've implemented this program, we use a checklist that makes it easy for Ambassadors to find a task they want to do. Some sample tasks:

As an Ambassador, I will:

• Identify and cultivate those in my circle of friends/ colleagues who would be interested in supporting our programs and services.

• Invite my best prospects to be my guests at appropriate functions, special tours of our facilities, regional activities.

• Help to steward relationships with our prospects and donors.

• Other:

When you've surveyed all of your board members, set up the information on a grid in which all board members have indicated what they want to do as Ambassadors (or Advocates or Askers). Then chart the responses so you can monitor their interests, follow up on assignments, and engage them in activities.

Keep the task list refreshed.

Even the most enthusiastic Ambassador will be looking for some new things to do. Put them in charge of an event. Create a board member mentoring program, and have them lead it. If yours is a membership organization, assign lists of new members to them for calling and outreach, regardless of the size of the gift. Give them responsibility for working with you to create a cultivation program leading up to a capital, endowment or annual campaign.

Meet with them as often as is feasible, and make sure at the annual meeting with the board member, that the board chair and the CEO discuss their list of Ambassador assignments and that successes are reviewed and appreciated.

•••

Fundraising isn't about money, it's about relationships. Ambassadors are the front line of relationship building. It'll serve your organization well to organize, acknowledge, and encourage as many board Ambassadors as you can.

36

Helping Board Members Become Advocates

In the previous chapter, I explored the role board members play as Ambassadors – part of a three-part series on creating "Triple A" boards comprised of Ambassadors, Advocates, and Askers. In this chapter, the focus is on board members who serve your organization as Advocates – both formal and informal.

If you'll recall, "AAA" boards are those where board members are offered opportunities to select from multiple assignments and the organization follows through by assigning and monitoring these tasks.

Because board members can avoid the things they don't like, the likelihood of them completing their assignments greatly increases.

Here, then, is what you should know to create the second "A" on your board – Advocates.

Advocates make the case.

In the last chapter, we said the simplest reduction of the Ambassadors' role was to make friends. The simplest expression of the Advocates' role is that they make the case. As a result, Advocates need to be better versed in the key features of your important work than those who are Ambassadors only. It is a slightly tougher role.

Advocates are connected to the constituencies you need.

While all board members bring connections, Advocates bring more conscious connections. Their work or community experience has put them into the active circle of opinion leaders or political leaders. Most often, it gives them pleasure to exercise these connections on your behalf – if they're adequately informed about what it is you want them to do and say.

Advocacy may be informal.

In the car pool, on the golf course, a well-coached advocate may informally plant seeds of interest or action on the part of people your organization wishes to engage.

Whatever the context or origin, Advocates will need to know what to say, and what you expect from the interaction. For example, you might ask them to sound someone out about their interest in a particular campaign or project, or you may want them to determine whether someone might be interested in possibly joining the board.

Keep in mind, however, that Advocates aren't asked to solicit or enlist at the time. Their job is to advance ideas and listen. And then report back to board or staff leadership.

Advocacy may be formal.

From time to time, all organizations need friends in high places: city hall, state legislature, Congress, or the national office of your local affiliate. For some people on your board this is a highly motivating task, allowing them to exercise their experience and connections in a way that brings them a sense of pride and accomplishment. Lobbying has its restrictions, of course – and this is not lobbying. It is simply finding the right people on your board to make a phone call or personal appearance during hearings, public sessions or others times when your organization's voice needs to be heard.

Whether informal or formal, Advocates need more than a nice story to tell.

Advocates benefit from the kind of coaching and training we provide for Askers. Points about cultivation and stewardship resonate well with the Advocates' role. And the aspects of the solicitation that have to do with presenting the case are particularly pertinent.

Short of engaging them in solicitation training, all advocates should be well-coached in handling objections and tough questions. Likewise, they should be clear about what you expect as an outcome of the conversation: information about what steps to take next, action on an issue that's critical to your planning or activities, or whom you should speak with next.

Advocates make good recruiters for your board – put them in key roles on your Committee on Trustees.

Advocates have a knack for putting a fine point on the key issues and opportunities your organization offers not only to donors and the community, but to potential board members. Engage them on this all-important committee.

Advocates like to cut to the chase.

While they should be good at telling stories that support the facts, Advocates are more likely to be educated or trained in getting to the purpose of the visit and not taking too much of people's time. Often, the time they have with a legislator – or in the car pool – is limited. They want to make the most of it.

Make sure you equip your Advocates with the facts they need, the stories to support those facts, the outcomes you anticipate, responses to the objections they may encounter, and expectations you have for next steps or delivery of information.

Although Askers get the attention when a big gift comes in, be sure to recognize the work of your Advocates in moving your vision and agenda in your community.

Often behind the scenes, Advocates don't get the recognition and peer applause Askers get. Don't fall into that trap. Make sure Advocates are singled out for their success in recruiting board members, forging a collaborative partnership with another nonprofit, making the case with a legislator or city council member, or successfully moving a reluctant funder into a position where an Asker was able to succeed in securing a gift.

The wave of the future will be closer collaboration with organizations addressing the same societal need – Advocates can serve you well here.

Egos and territories should have no place in our sector, but they abound. Collaborations and partnerships require compromise and giving up ground that may initially feel too hallowed to release.

Advocates, because they are coached in the purpose and outcomes of their assignments are able to stay the course, often becoming champions at compromise in working with two or more organizations for the best possible organizational alignment.

Recently, in northeastern Ohio, eight land trusts merged to become "Western Reserve Land Conservancy"(WRLC) – a regional entity that aims to protect forests, farms, wetlands and other natural areas in a 14-county area along the shores of Lake Erie. In their press release, an unknown source was quoted as saying, "It's easier to put a man on the moon than to merge nonprofits." And yet, in a conversation with Lauri Gross, media relations staffer with WRLC, she cited the advocacy role of board members of these organizations as extremely valuable in effecting the merger.

According to the press release, board members saw that it "was about the land" and that a merged organization would ultimately have more leveraging power and be more effective.

If an Advocate on your board is also gifted as a speaker, utilize those talents at service clubs, churches, and other gatherings.

Public speaking is not every Advocate's key strength, but many of them can represent you well at community meetings. Of course, it's a good idea to review the speech before it's delivered; and also to have someone from the organization's leadership attend the talk (at least at first). You may, after a time, develop such confidence in your Advocates that review and attendance is not necessary.

•••

Advocates work well for us both behind the scenes and in leadership roles in the community. Be sure you think carefully through the many ways they can be involved on your behalf, and prepare a checklist for board members that offers them multiple ways to support you in their advocacy. Remember that some board members will have their own "AAA Rating" – they will do all three. Others may do one or two.

37

The Dynamics of Successful Board Meetings

Do your board members look forward to board meetings? No, I'm not joking. There are actually organizations where board members *like* attending board meetings. They find them stimulating and motivating.

But sadly, this seems to be the exception.

More common is the experience of a high-profile, much-sought-after board member who resigned after his first meeting. He specifically cited the dynamics of the board meeting as the reason for his departure. It was, in his words, "just not for him."

Another individual, a busy entrepreneur, recently said he'd never join another board because it was only about talk, talk, talk. No action. And, therefore, not his "cup of tea."

Across all kinds of organizations, the attitude of board members towards attending board meetings runs the gamut from *dread* to *endure* to *duty* to *enjoyment*. Where would your organization fit on this scale?

If you want your board members to look forward to the experience, here's what you should know about the dynamics of successful meetings.

Something is accomplished.

That may sound obvious, but beyond talk, too little is accomplished at many board meetings. To stay energized, people need a sense of completion and closure on important items. If you don't have a quorum, no decisions can be made. Worse, even with a quorum there may be no decisions to make. Why come to a board meeting, then?

Be sure you have action items on your agenda and that they're acted on. And, be certain to report on the results of actions board members have taken previously.

People are heard.

If the *real* board meeting takes place in the parking lot or on cell phones *after* the meeting, then you should look into the way discussion is handled during the meeting.

Are there a few who dominate to the exclusion of others? Are new ideas welcome, or are they dismissed with the tired bromide, "We tried that and it didn't work"?

If people have issues, is there a process to ensure that the issue is placed on the board agenda and a well-facilitated discussion takes place?

When people can participate fully at a meeting, their engagement increases. When they're ignored or shut down, they detach from the meeting and, in many cases, from the organization.

The meeting is well-run.

Does your chair know how to run a meeting, or does she need some coaching?

Most communities have management support organizations that coach people in running better meetings. It would be worth the investment to send not only your board chair, but all committee chairs as well.

There is a generous exposure to mission, not just administrative concerns.

Every board meeting should have a "mission moment" – a five-minute session in the middle of the meeting where you hear from a client, grateful patient, music student, alum, parent, or whoever can speak with passion about the impact of your organization in their lives. Do this in the middle of the meeting to catch the latecomers and the early-departers.

Reports by program staff don't carry the same passion and authenticity. You need to hear it from the source.

There are opportunities for site visits.

Whatever your service, think of ways to get your board members into the place where the work happens – at least once a year.

If your organization's work isn't something outsiders can observe (mental health, prison work, medical programs with at-risk patients), then take board members to the site and have a presentation from physicians or other relevant experts about the latest breakthroughs in research, treatment, or care.

Let them see the facility and meet the staff, even if they can't watch the work. Board members connect in new ways when they have this experience.

Board members have fun, and there is an appreciation of good humor.

Our work is serious, but that doesn't mean board meetings can't be fun. Encourage humor and interaction. Shared laughter deepens engagement.

Board meeting dynamics that are relaxed, warm, and accepting have a powerful effect on members, diminishing their sense of reserve and allowing humor and ease of expression to emerge.

One organization I'm familiar with recently completed a marketing and fundraising DVD in which board members were interviewed. At the board meeting, instead of playing the finished product, an "outtake" DVD was shown ... with hilarious results. The real DVD then followed.

Successes are shared.

Beginning the meeting with an SOS (Share Our Success) session is a great way to start people thinking about their interaction with the organization.

At first, the board chair will probably have to ask some members before the meeting to share a story of a solicitation, a meeting, a random conversation in which there was, for example, unsolicited praise for the organization.

After a few meetings, once board members see this as a constructive measure, the challenge will be to keep the SOS stories to a limit.

Meeting logistics are clear and observed.

Start on time. Keep the agenda moving. And if the usual length of the meeting has to be extended because of a serious item of business, let people know in advance and discuss the extension at the beginning of the board meeting.

The boardroom environment is conducive to doing business.

Except for the site-based gathering, board meetings should

be held in the organization's boardroom if there is one, or in another facility with a board meeting area that's conducive to maintaining a professional image.

Gone are the days when organizations needed to look poor to raise money. Now, we realize that the confidence people place in an organization is the basis of their investment. Their confidence is compromised when they're brought to a shabby facility.

They understand that their job is governance, not management.

This distinction makes all the difference in the dynamics of board meetings. It keeps board members at the right level of discussion, and (hopefully) prevents them from sinking into the mire of management issues belonging to the staff. The focus on governance is established through the agenda and the items emphasized.

It is also a result of keeping the detail work – including work with the staff on operational issues – to committees and letting the outcomes of those meetings be reported as a framework for making quality governance decisions – decisions on policies, strategies, and evaluation.

•••

Effective board meeting dynamics are a surprisingly important point for overall board member satisfaction. Good meetings energize, inform, and inspire enthusiasm for service.

If attendance at your board meetings has declined, evaluate the quality and dynamics of your meetings. Maybe people have checked out because the meetings were so deadly dull, contentious, or meaningless. Fortunately, with the above suggestions in mind, this problem is relatively easy to remedy.

267

38

Keeping Your Board And Staff Partnership In Balance

The nonprofit sector is built on partnerships. We're partners with the community in solving problems and enhancing the quality of life. We initiate partnerships with funders for the mutual accomplishment of our mission, and with volunteers to help us leverage time and money in the most effective way possible. The dual leadership structure of nonprofits, in which board and staff share responsibility for the organization, is itself a preeminent nonprofit partnership.

Maintaining a balanced environment in which partnerships flourish can be challenging. But it is worth the effort. Here's what you should know about keeping your board-staff partnership in balance.

Be sure board and staff have a shared vision and that they understand how that vision will be achieved.

The heart of all successful partnerships, and the fulcrum for maintaining balance, is a shared vision. If it's been a while since your organization voiced its vision, make that a top priority at a retreat or other forum.

When board and staff members come together to create and commit to a shared vision, they become energized around their areas of common agreement and it becomes easier to delineate their respective roles.

Be sure both board and staff are involved in strategic planning.

Whatever planning approach you use, be sure both board and staff are full participants in the process and in the ultimate ownership of the plan. Nothing throws a board-staff partnership off balance more dramatically than plans generated by either board or staff without adequate input from the other.

If you do your planning at an annual retreat, make sure it is a *board-staff* retreat. Excluding one of the partners is the best way to undermine a partnership. Exclusion builds suspicion and mistrust and leads to "border crossing," that is, the tendency of boards and staffs to cross into each other's territory because they feel shut off from the vision and the process of setting goals and objectives.

Define board and staff roles clearly and often.

All staff members should have written job descriptions. So should all volunteers, including board members. When provided with a written job description, board members view their responsibilities more seriously.

In addition to their own job descriptions, board members should be provided with the job descriptions of the key individuals with whom they'll be working (administrative, development, and program leaders). They should also be given job descriptions for the committees to which they've been assigned.

With this information in hand, board members get a better idea of their role and a greater sense of being a partner with staff in the mutual achievement of the organization's mission.

Set mutual expectations and evaluate often.

In addition to job descriptions, which outline individual and committee responsibilities, it's a good idea annually to share expectations among board and staff leadership. Daily, we evaluate people on our expectations of them. But too often they don't know what those expectations are.

Expectations and responsibilities are linked, but different. A board member's responsibility may be to attend board meetings regularly. But, the expectation of the executive director may be that board materials will have been read and that meetings will start on time. Irritation can lead to strife.

An annual setting of expectations is a good idea. And, facilitated well, this session needn't be dreaded. It's merely a chance to let board say to staff what their expectations are, and for staff to relay theirs to the board.

Evaluation of volunteers and an annual board self-evaluation also keep the partnership strong and in balance.

Revisit the mission at every opportunity.

The mission is why you exist as an organization. It is the community need you're meeting. It is the glue binding board and staff members together. It is the inspiration for dealing with the mundane and for stretching to do the exceptional. To revisit it isn't to re-read a statement: it is to witness firsthand the impact of your organization's work in the community.

It's easy for staff and board to become so consumed with

service delivery or with generating resources that they lose sight of the impact they're having.

You'll create stronger partnerships and keep the momentum brisk by continually presenting to both board and staff the intertwined nature of what each does. The board generates financial resources, which provide staff with what they need to do their job, which in turn has an impact on the community – the full cycle of which makes the job of raising money much easier for board members.

Keep both board and staff connected with that impact. Invite those who have benefited to tell their stories. This kind of "product demonstration" is a highly effective way to keep the sense of partnership and maintain balance. Each person feels as though his or her role is important because the results are so apparent.

Create an environment of mutual respect.

Commitment to board-staff partnerships is a philosophical issue, and the major manifestation of such a commitment is an environment characterized by mutual respect for staff and volunteers.

Because volunteer involvement is mandated in our sector (hence, the term "voluntary sector"), the absence of visible commitment to a true partnership is sometimes an invitation for boards to circle the wagons and become a divisive force. They step into areas where staff doesn't want them, principally because they've been denied a role in the areas where they could be effective.

Mutual respect is created (or recreated) when this issue is dealt with, when board-staff roles are clearly defined, and when appropriate avenues for board (and other volunteer) involvement are delineated.

Watch for symptoms of mission drift.

Mission drift is serious. It's a result of an erosion of the board-staff partnership. Its symptoms are those of an organization out of balance. The symptoms are:

• Board meetings in which there's little or no mention of the programs or services except in the financial report.

• Board members who refuse to get involved with the organization except at board meetings and make little or no financial commitment.

• Leaders who fail to encourage leadership growth and succession.

• Battles for control between board and staff.

• A shift from the passionate commitment that characterizes board membership in its early stages to an overly pragmatic view often found among board members in organizations with greater maturity.

Reward teamwork.

It's important to reward and recognize individual achievements among board and staff members who fulfill their roles well. It's equally important to verbally and visibly reward teamwork. When projects, programs, or events are the result of effective partnerships working in balance, let that be known. Cite the efforts that were made to include staff and volunteers, and emphasize the way in which each fulfilled their defined roles.

Make sure the reward and recognition you offer is framed by the shared vision and the way in which the achievement or event supports that vision. Stress the impact it will have on the organization and the community.

Set standards and adhere to them.

Most people who become involved as staff and board leaders

want standards. They want accountability. They want to be evaluated. They are inspired by a commitment to quality and excellence, and will advance that commitment through their own work if the standards are set.

Often, we erode the partnership balance by not setting standards. If your organization is important to the community, then the work of staff and volunteers must be of the best quality. Convey that. It will instill a culture of pride and help ensure the highest performance by everyone.

Communicate openly and often regarding progress, challenges, and opportunities.

Partnerships and balance wither when either board or staff feels they're kept in the dark about policies, operations, or other issues. Establish regular communication avenues between board and staff and guard against an "us and them" culture. The more personal the communication, the more effective.

Engage board and staff informally between meetings. Brown bag discussion sessions and other opportunities to focus on issues relevant to the organization increase the sense of trust and partnership. For example, invite staff and board for casual meetings with a visiting professional or discuss a pertinent issue in the community that could have an impact on program or services. Another effective approach is to circulate "draft" documents for board comment.

•••

Investing in strategies to keep board-staff roles balanced, and to keep partnerships strong, is a critical function of healthy nonprofits. These suggestions will I hope help your organization maintain balanced relationships and a focus on mission.

39

Setting Boundaries For Board Involvement

We all want our boards to be involved. We urge their partnership in donor development and fundraising. We applaud their role in stewardship. We love their service on committees, and encourage their leadership in the community. We convince them to be our ambassadors and advocates, and seek their counsel on a wide variety of issues.

Then, one day, we find ourselves knocking heads over something they should *not* be involved in, and realize our board has moved from supportive involvement to inappropriate intervention. There's been a shift from governing to managing.

Here's what you should know about preventing this problematic shift and correcting the imbalance when it occurs.

Be a great communicator.

My observations over the years lead me to believe that more communication is always better than less. When people don't know what's going on, they *imagine* what's going on. If you don't tell them your progress, they assume there is none.

If your board is teetering on the brink of over-involvement, feeling they must generate *some* activity, consider sending weekly summaries of all the news. Use email, fax or snail mail: whatever they're used to receiving. Keep the bullet points crisp and mix narrative and quantitative information. When they realize progress is being made, their urge to intervene will diminish.

Create a feedback system for questions and responses.

The absence of a feedback system can cause inappropriate intervention by those who feel out of the loop. If people are frustrated at not being heard in a meeting, they may well make themselves heard with negative comments in the community. Or, they may do an "end run" around the executive director and complain to other senior staff or board members.

Establish and adhere to timelines the board is aware of and wants to see completed.

We can waste a lot of time answering six phone calls from board members who want to know when the annual fund materials will be ready.

We can become frustrated and impatient over capital campaign volunteers who repeatedly want to know the status of a call for which they're preparing or the results of one already completed.

We can also derail many meeting agendas by failing to communicate progress prior to the meeting.

When timelines aren't communicated, the next thing you know, board members are jumping in to see that the job gets done. If that's not what you want, then let them know things are under control.

Be sure board and committee members understand their responsibilities.

This sounds so obvious you may be wondering why I've included it. But it's precisely because it's so obvious that we overlook it.

Dust off your board and committee job descriptions and the statements of individual board and committee member responsibilities. Be sure they're part of an annual orientation for all board and committee members. Review the responsibilities and be sure people agree to them.

Be certain board and committee members understand how staff responsibilities balance with theirs in all the areas where they partner.

We talk a great deal about board-staff partnerships. We know that when they're in synch, more things get done and everyone feels good about how they get done.

In your board and committee orientations, list specifically what the staff is responsible for and what the board is expected to do. This includes everything from financial matters to fundraising to personnel issues, and more. When the boundaries are known, volunteers are less apt to step over them.

Be sure staff members carry out their responsibilities: when a leadership void is sensed, board members will fill it.

When board members sense a lack of progress, it's either because we don't communicate it to them, or we're not doing what needs to be done.

Staff members have a formidable role to play in maintaining the right balance between board involvement and intervention. It's imperative they carry out what's expected of them and communicate the results to the board members with whom they work. If they don't, board members, because they have legal and fiduciary responsibility for the organization, are apt to step in.

For example, when board members don't get financial reports on a timely basis, they may begin showing up in the finance office to offer suggestions about form and deadlines. If the financial officer doesn't want this kind of help, she needs to be more diligent about the reports and the cycle.

In general, board members who care deeply and passionately about the organization will want to rush in to fill a leadership void if they sense there is one. Stop the void from occurring.

Resolve boundary issues before they grow and permeate the culture.

Intervention unchecked can easily become the organizational culture. Before you know it, the board has shifted from governance to management. Watch for the danger signals and realign the boundaries before the behavior permeates your organization.

In one start-up organization, several board members decided not only to hire the CEO but to have final approval on the next tier of administrative employees as well. The CEO said no, that it was her responsibility to hire those who reported to her. She would be happy for them to meet with final candidates, but the decision would be hers.

It was an important step in keeping the board in balance and establishing the role of the CEO at the outset.

In another organization, several key leaders from the board decided that a particular employee, who reported to the executive director, wasn't who they wanted in that position. On their own, they identified and interviewed another candidate and then instructed the executive director to hire that person to supervise the existing employee.

Had the board not backed off, and if this serious level of intervention by the board had continued, the CEO would have had to confront the board chair and the executive committee about reestablishing boundaries.

Know when board member intervention is needed, and what to do afterwards to get things back on track.

Boards rush in – and should – when there's a scandal involving the CEO or other key person, a financial setback or disaster that rocks the organization, a serious breach of ethics, or a death affecting the organization deeply.

Ultimately, the board bears legal and fiduciary responsibility and they should intervene and assume increased responsibility when emergencies arise. However, the first goal of such intervention should be to restore the balance with effective staff leadership.

It is critical that board members resist the temptation of staying in a quasi-administrative role once a problem has been solved. They should continue to monitor the situation, but must return control to the organization's staff as soon as possible.

To prevent excessive intervention, be firm, avoid defensive behavior, and reaffirm the strength of both partners in the board-staff relationship.

It's easy to feel upset and frustrated when board members get overly involved. It's also easy to become defensive when it looks like board members are moving into areas of your responsibility and asking you repeated questions. Neither of these behaviors is particularly productive.

Go back to the basics: communicate progress and setbacks; perform at your highest level; state board and committee responsibilities clearly; define the way the board-staff partnership should work; give and encourage feedback; and be open to suggestions.

Although sometimes it may seem so, few board members want to make a career of what we do – they just want to feel as though they're partners in our success.

•••

Get your board involved. Better yet, get them engaged. But remember that your best role will be to clearly communicate their responsibilities and live up to yours. That will help keep the board-staff relationship and duties balanced so there is mutual respect, trust, and a shared expectation that the job will get done without inappropriate board intervention.

40

Organizing a Successful Board Retreat

Whether your organization has a tradition of an annual board retreat, or is considering one for the first time, there are a number of approaches and practices that'll help your retreat be more productive, relevant, and enjoyable.

Often based around institutional or development planning and evaluation, and frequently held at a site away from your usual meeting facility, retreats offer a unique opportunity for board and staff members to get to know one another and the organization better. Because retreats are longer than regular board meetings, there's time to focus on mission, vision, and values, rather than just on reports and action items.

A successful board retreat can be a catalyst for change and here's what you should know about organizing one.

You may have to do a selling job to get your board members to buy-in.

If it's the first time you've attempted to organize a board retreat -- or if previous retreats have been viewed as a waste –

there may be mild to severe resistance from the board. This is especially true if board commitment is uneven and leadership is skeptical of the importance of an extended session. Convincing boards it's vital for them to spend four hours (the minimum time for a "retreat") to three days (probably the maximum time) may be a challenge.

Encourage discussion of the retreat idea at a board meeting, and gain the broadest possible consensus. Then, develop a solid outcomes-focused agenda to lure these committed but very busy people, and send out a notice stating:

• Why the retreat is important at this time (for example, a change in the funding base, need to evaluate the market for services, potential for new funding),

• What the principal goals are (for example, setting the groundwork for a new long-range plan or a development plan of action),

• The process that will be used to achieve the goals (presentations, facilitated discussions, small group meetings), and,

• Why board participation is key to the retreat's success.

The first time out, aim for a short good retreat and gradually, over the years, extend the time as the need demands.

Be inclusive when developing the list of who will attend.

In addition to board members, include key administrative, development, and program staff to ensure clarity and continuity in fulfilling any plans devised at the retreat. Small organizations in which there may be much shared responsibility between board and staff often include the entire staff.

There are exceptions, of course. Some board retreats are called for the express purpose of addressing key staffing issues which may involve the executive director. In these cases, the retreat usually begins with an executive session with only board members in attendance. When their business is finished, the executive director or other staff members are invited to discuss the results of the board deliberations and to begin working towards implementing changes. Needless to say, these latter kinds of retreats are tough, tense meetings.

Fortunately, the vast majority of board retreats aren't grim gatherings at which sensitive personnel issues are resolved. Most are great opportunities for exploring issues and ideas in a relaxed environment and for spending time getting to know each other.

Enlist a retreat planning committee whose members represent those who will attend.

Committee members become the principal advocates for the retreat, so they must represent both board and staff if both will be included in the retreat. They need to be clear and consistent in conveying the importance of the meeting and the anticipated outcomes to others. During the ramp-up period, give the committee chair time on board and staff agendas.

Allow ample time for the planning committee to develop the agenda, make the arrangements, organize the program, and build in activities to help people become better acquainted.

Planning should begin three to four months before the retreat. If yours is an annual retreat, it should be done the same month each year, and be built into the regular board meeting calendar.

The committee should establish preliminary desired outcomes and submit a tentative agenda to the board at least three months before the anticipated retreat. Include the facilitator (see below) in the planning meetings to the extent possible. She needs to understand the dynamics and the issues. Provide the facilitator with a list of the outcomes you want (she may want to prepare the initial agenda).

Supply the committee with notes and minutes from past retreats. If this is your first, it's helpful for someone from the committee to be connected with a board or staff member from another organization that's experienced with board retreats.

Be sure the agenda mixes information, inspiration, and motivation.

There are three frames for organizing a retreat: there are also three important outcomes.

Inspiration is provided by bringing the "product" to the retreat. One retreat succeeded in persuading reluctant board members to become active in a stalled capital campaign by bringing in three grant recipients of the fund the organization was trying to expand. Each person spoke of the impact the scholarships had made on their lives, and thanked board and staff members for making it possible for them to achieve their personal and professional goals.

Information is another critical ingredient. Be sure the facts are current, accurate, and presented in a form which stimulates discussion and can be used by board and staff members as they connect with others in the community.

Motivation is, like the others, both an ingredient and an outcome. People are motivated to be advocates for an organization when there's a feeling of confidence that their efforts will be valued and make a difference. This part of the retreat is locked in when program or administrative staff convey to the development staff and to board members how critical their efforts are to the capacity of the organization to meet community needs.

Motivation is also stimulated by having each retreat participant, at the end of the session, voice their commitment to the outcomes generated at the retreat.

Seek 100 percent attendance; be happy with 85 percent; cancel if only 70 percent sign up.

It simply isn't worth the effort and cost (place, facilitator, refreshments) if too few people participate. Early notice of the date, sensitivity to the length of the meeting, and the distance participants may have to travel can also improve attendance. Use a call-down process by committee members to reconfirm attendance two weeks to 10 days before the retreat. If there's dramatic falloff, have the board chair or executive director call each board person. If that doesn't work, consider cancellation.

Decide early in your planning if you'll use an inside or outside facilitator.

Inside facilitators come without cost, but may lack the required objectivity. The advantage of an outside facilitator is professional skill and the objectivity to move the meeting along and not get tangled up in politics or difficult relationships. The principal disadvantage is cost ($300 to $1500 or more a day).

If you choose to use an outside facilitator, it's a good idea to have a backup just in case conflicts arise. Involve the facilitator in the retreat planning: don't bring her in cold.

Disarm all potentially explosive individuals and issues before the retreat or, if that's not possible, be sure the facilitator and the participants are aware of the situation.

Potentially explosive individuals or issues may find their way into the retreat. These land mines have exploded the agenda of more than one well-planned retreat. When the facilitator, committee, and participants are aware of the danger spots and of people who may have volatility around certain issues, there's opportunity to be sensitive and hopefully use the retreat as a forum for building consensus and shared vision.

A skillful facilitator can sometimes bring these issues to the surface within the context of a larger discussion and in such a way that they're addressed objectively, and tensions are neutralized.

As the retreat approaches, keep the reminders and the information flowing.

One week before the retreat, send out a final package with directions to the site, advice about dress, information about the facility ("bring your swim suit or tennis racket"), final agenda/ schedule, and any last minute background reading materials or other information needed to enhance the agenda.

Have solid closure to the retreat.

Much happens during a retreat, whether it's four hours or three days. Friendships are made. Tensions arise or are resolved. Plans are made or revised. Information is given and digested. There is time for reflection and comment.

Organizations miss an opportunity to further increase the impact of a retreat when they end the session in a haphazard way, with people drifting out with little understanding of the next steps or the purpose of their participation.

Allow enough time at the end of the retreat to do several things: A) Confirm the next steps, including timeline, for any planning that has been done; B) Make commitments; C) Have the facilitator give her closing observations; and D) End with a short "stem winder" from a board member, staff leader, or the facilitator.

In the follow up letter to each participant, thank them for their contribution to the retreat and their commitment, summarize the outcomes of the session, recount some of the moments that were fun and memorable, recap the next steps, and include complete notes from the retreat.

This information should also be sent to those who couldn't attend, with a cover letter expressing the importance of the outcomes and the way they can participate now in implementing the decisions.

•••

Retreats that lack this thorough planning and follow-up may be viewed by participants as isolated and time consuming experiences. By implementing these suggestions, you'll be more likely to have a successful retreat that will engage both board and staff while it's happening and ensure their continued commitment to its outcomes long after it's over.

AFTERWORD

Going over goal means much more than raising more money than you had hoped. It means exceeding your aspirations for impact, involvement, and visibility.

Ultimately, your community, not your organization, is the end user of the money you raise. It simply isn't about you. It's about those you serve and those who give their time and treasure to make sure your theater company thrives, your programs for seniors increase with rising demand, your health initiatives respond to growing urgency, and your educational offerings stimulate curiosity and satisfy the urge to know.

The array of ideas in this book mirrors the array of opportunities you have to express new goals that go far beyond financial. Set and exceed a goal for growing your board's willingness to get involved in donor development and fundraising. Convey and achieve new aspirations for creating a dynamic strategic plan. Build and successfully implement an agenda for engaging younger board members and for creating a stronger culture of philanthropy. Aim for and attain new heights in the quality and impact of your marketing.

When you set these goals, your financial goals will be easier to meet. You'll excel not only at fundraising, but at so many of the truly important success markers for our sector: visibility, impact, community engagement, and trust.

Set your goals. Aim high. And always remember that those goals aren't just about money, they are about creating the environment in which staff, volunteers, donors, and others feel a part of your vision and are resolute in their commitment to help you achieve it. They are about engaging the community in your mission and securing strong relationships for the future. And they are about sustainability – that quality of effective organizations that gives them the power and drive to continually create the capacity that moves them towards an envisioned future.

Some of the ideas in this book require changing the way you do things. Good. We resist change because, in the words of one of my colleagues, we learn to do the wrong things well. Learn, instead, to do the right things well. Take risks. Breathe in new ideas and master new approaches – then you'll be able to set large goals that inspire.

As a sector we are change agents and yet we resist change. There are ideas in this book that I hope have prodded your imagination. I hope they will energize you and give you the inspiration to do things in new ways.

Remember, if there were no change, there would be no butterflies.

The Gold Standard
In Books for Nonprofit Boards

Each can be read in an hour • *Quantity discounts up to 50 percent*

Fund Raising Realities Every Board Member Must Face
David Lansdowne, 112 pp., $24.95, ISBN 1889102105

If every board member of every nonprofit organization in America read this book, it's no exaggeration to say that millions upon millions of additional dollars would be raised.

How could it be otherwise when, after spending just *one* hour with this gem, board members everywhere would understand virtually everything they need to know about raising major gifts. Not more, not less. Just exactly what they need to do to be successful.

In his book, *Fund Raising Realities Every Board Member Must Face: A 1-Hour Crash Course on Raising Major Gifts for Nonprofit Organizations*, David Lansdowne has distilled the essence of major gifts fund raising, put it in the context of 47 "realities," and delivered it in unfailingly clear prose.

Nothing about this book will intimidate board members. It is brief, concise, easy to read, and free of all jargon. Further, it is a work that motivates, showing as it does just how doable raising big money is.

Asking   Jerold Panas, 112 pp., $24.95, ISBN 1889102172

It ranks right up there with public speaking. Nearly all of us fear it. And yet it is critical to our success. Asking for money. It makes even the stout-hearted quiver.

But now comes a book, *Asking: A 59-Minute Guide to Everything Board Members, Staff and Volunteers Must Know to Secure the Gift*. And short of a medical elixir, it's the next best thing for emboldening you, your board members and volunteers to ask with skill, finesse … and powerful results.

Jerold Panas, who as a staff person, board member and volunteer has secured gifts ranging from $50 to $50 million, understands the art of asking perhaps better than anyone in America.

He knows what makes donors tick, he's intimately familiar with the anxieties of board members, and he fully understands the frustrations and demands of staff.

He has harnessed all of this knowledge and experience and produced a landmark book. What *Asking* convincingly shows — and one reason staff will applaud the book and board members will devour it — is that it doesn't take stellar communication skills to be an effective asker.

Nearly everyone, regardless of their persuasive ability, can become an effective fundraiser if they follow a few step-by-step guidelines.

Emerson & Church, Publishers

Big Gifts for Small Groups
Andy Robinson, 112 pp., $24.95, ISBN 1889102210

If yours is among the tens of thousands of organizations for whom six- and seven-figure gifts are unattainable, then Andy Robinson's book, *Big Gifts for Small Groups*, is just the ticket for you and your board.

Robinson is the straightest of shooters and there literally isn't one piece of advice in this book that's glib or inauthentic. As a result of Robinson's 'no bull' style, board members will instantly take to the book, confident the author isn't slinging easy bromides.

They'll learn everything they need to know from this one-hour read: how to get ready for the campaign, who to approach, where to find them; where to conduct the meeting, what to bring with you, how to ask, how to make it easy for the donor to give, what to do once you have the commitment – even how to convey your thanks in a memorable way.

Believing that other books already focus on higher sum gifts, the author wisely targets a range that's been neglected: $500 to $5,000.

Robinson has a penchant for good writing and for using precisely the right example or anecdote to illustrate his point. But more importantly he lets his no-nonsense personality shine through. The result being that by the end of the book, board members just may turn to one another and say, "Hey, we can do this" – and actually mean it.

How Are We Doing? Gayle Gifford, 120 pp., $24.95, ISBN 1889102237

Ah, simplicity.

That's not a word usually voiced in the same breath as 'board evaluation.' Or brevity … and clarity … and cogency.

Yet all four aptly describe Gayle Gifford's book, *How Are We Doing: A 1-Hour Guide to Evaluating Your Performance as a Nonprofit Board*.

Until now, almost all books dealing with board evaluation have had an air of unreality about them. The perplexing graphs, the matrix boxes, the overlong questionnaires. It took only a thumbing through to render a judgment: "My board's going to use this? Get real!"

Enter Gayle Gifford. Inhale the fresh air. See the ground break. Watch the clutter clear. Gifford has pioneered an elegantly simple and enjoyable way for boards to evaluate *and* improve their overall performance.

It all comes down to answering some straightforward questions – questions that, as Graham Greene would say, get to "the heart of the matter."

It doesn't matter whether the setting is formal or casual, whether you have 75 board members or seven, or whether yours is an established institution or a grassroots start-up. All that matters is that the questions are answered candidly and the responses discussed. It doesn't get any easier, or more refreshing, than that.

Emerson & Church, Publishers

The Fundraising Habits of Supremely Successful Boards
Jerold Panas, 108 pp., $24.95, ISBN 1889102261

Over the course of a storied career, Jerold Panas has worked with literally thousands of boards, from those governing the toniest of prep schools to those spearheading the local Y. He has counseled floundering groups; he has been the wind beneath the wings of boards whose organizations have soared.

In fact, it's a safe bet that Panas has observed more boards at work than perhaps anyone in America, all the while helping them to surpass their campaign goals of $100,000 to $100 million.

Funnel every ounce of that experience and wisdom into a single book and what you end up with is *The Fundraising Habits of Supremely Successful Boards*, the brilliant culmination of what Panas has learned firsthand about boards who excel at the task of resource development.

Fundraising Habits offers a panoply of habits any board would be wise to cultivate. Some are specific, with measurable outcomes. Others are more intangible, with Panas seeking to impart an attitude of success.

In all, there are 25 habits and each is explored in two- and three-page chapters ... all of them animated by real-life stories only this grandmaster of philanthropy can tell.

Fund Raising Mistakes that Bedevil All Boards (& Staff Too)
Kay Sprinkel Grace, 112 pp., $24.95, ISBN 1889102229

Fundraising mistakes are a thing of the past. Or, rather, there's no excuse for making one anymore. If you blunder from now on, it's simply evidence you haven't read Kay Grace's book, in which she exposes *all* of the costly errors that thwart us time and again.

Some, like the following, will be second nature to you, but not to your board for whom this book is intended:
- "Tax deductibility is a powerful incentive." It isn't, as you know.
- "People will give just because yours is a good cause." They won't.
- "Wealth is mostly what determines a person's willingness to give." Not really. Other factors are equally important.

Other mistakes aren't as readily apparent. For example: "You need a powerful board to have a successful campaign." Truth be told, many are convinced that without an influential board they can't succeed. Grace shows otherwise.

Then, too, there are more nuanced mistakes:
- "We can't raise big money - we don't
know any rich people." Don't believe it. You can raise substantial dollars.
- "Without a stable of annual donors, you can't have a successful capital campaign." In fact you can, but your tactics will be different.
- "You need a feasibility study before launching a capital campaign." Turns out, you might not.

Emerson & Church, Publishers

Great Boards for Small Groups
Andy Robinson, 112 pp., $24.95, ISBN 1889102040

Yours is a good board, but you want it to be better.
• You want clearly defined objectives …
• Meetings with more focus …
• Broader participation in fundraising …
• And more follow-through between meetings.
You want these and a dozen other tangibles and intangibles that will propel your board from good to great. Say hello to your guide, Andy Robinson, who has a real knack for offering "forehead-slapping" solutions – "Of course! Why haven't we been doing this?"

Take what he calls the "Fundraising Menu." Here, board members are asked to generate a list of all the ways (direct and indirect) they could assist in fundraising. The list is prioritized and then used to help each trustee prepare a personalized fundraising agreement meeting his specific needs.

Simple, right? Yet the Fundraising Menu is the closest thing you'll find to guaranteeing a board's commitment to raising money.

Great Boards for Small Groups contains 31 brief chapters. In fact the whole book can be read in an hour. Funny thing, its impact on those who heed its advice will last for years.

The Ultimate Board Member's Book
Kay Sprinkel Grace, 114 pp., $24.95, ISBN 1889102180

Here is a book for *all* of your board members:
• Those needing an orientation to the unique responsibilities of a nonprofit board,
• Those wishing to clarify exactly what their individual role is,
• Those hoping to fulfill their charge with maximum effectiveness.

Kay Sprinkel Grace's perceptive work will take board members just one hour to read, and yet they'll come away from *The Ultimate Board Member's Book* with a firm command of just what they need to do to help your organization succeed.

It's all here in 114 tightly organized and jargon-free pages: how boards work, what the job entails, the time commitment involved, the role of staff, serving on committees and task forces, fundraising responsibilities, conflicts of interest, group decision-making, effective recruiting, de-enlisting board members, board self-evaluation, and more.

In sum, everything a board member needs to know to serve knowledgeably is here.

The Ultimate Board Member's Book is 'real world,' not theoretical, concrete not abstract. It focuses on the issues and concerns that all board members will inevitably face.

Emerson & Church, Publishers

INDEX